The Secret Child

Reviews from www.Amazon.com:

"I was intrigued from the first words of the first chapter. Kirsten tells her story in such an honest and compelling way that you will not want to put it down! Her humor shines through even in the painful events that shaped her life. I came away with inspiration and a desire to realize my true identity. A must read!"

"I loved this book. Kirsten has done a great job telling her story. This story will touch your life and help you cherish those around you. You will cry and you will cheer. Kirsten's amazing story is just beginning. She is full of talent and is surrounded by a great husband, boys, family and an incredible God. This is just the beginning for sure. Watch out world, this is one special lady."

"Kirsten did an incredible job writing her biography. I felt as if I was walking the journey with her. Her love for the Lord, her maternal mother, her husband and sons and her adoptive parents is incredible. A very easy read and once you start reading, you won't put it down. Cannot wait for another book by Kirsten!"

"Wanted to let you know that I downloaded your book to my Kindle for Martha to read. She started it Wednesday and was finished yesterday. She loved it, said to tell you congratulations on it, and can't wait until the next one is available. Your story makes her want to investigate my background as my parents divorced when I was very small and I never knew my father or any of his children from a later marriage. Thanks for telling your story."

The Secret Child

By
Kirsten Hart

Chapter One

Some surprises I like. Others I don't. Unexpected cards, flowers, and gifts I do like. I have absolutely no problem with accepting those kinds of surprises. Love. Absolutely love surprise gifts. Especially when it's something I've wanted but didn't want to spend family money to buy.

Sometimes there are bad surprises. A flat tire. A car that won't start. The unexpected death of a loved one. Finding out that your job has been terminated, or hearing that you have a life threatening illness would be a surprise that is shocking and life changing.

I had a life changing surprise the summer of 2007. My surprise came in the form of a phone call. I'll never forget the phone message. It changed my life. I've heard it said that one phone call can change your life. It's true.

My phone call came after my husband and I had been asked to lead music for a Christian cruise to Mexico. How fun. Everything would be taken care of for us, and the only thing we needed to do was to make sure we had current passports. Easy enough.

I found my husband Dave's certificate, and both birth certificates for our boys, but mine was no where to be found. After digging through every drawer and box in the house, I decided it had to be somewhere out in the garage. We were under a time crunch, and had to get our passports processed as soon as possible.

We were living in Houston, Texas, and were in the delightful month of July. Have you been in Houston in July? The heat and humidity is almost unbearable. With zero certificate locating results inside, I ventured forth into our garage continuing the search. We had moved the year prior, and still had a few packed boxes that were full of papers that you had to keep, but didn't necessarily need to access on a daily basis. After sweating, searching, and killing multiple bugs, I decided there had to be a better and easier option. I went online, and searched the words 'copy of birth certificate'. I found out that for only thirty-five dollars, I could order a copy of my birth certificate online, and have it in my hands by the end of the week. Easy enough. I filled out the online form, and hit the enter key. Done.

The next morning, while checking my messages, I received a message from the city where I was born. This was my life changing call. The woman speaking was from the health records office in Rochester, New York. As I listened to her message, I became slightly numb.

"I'm sorry, Mrs. Hart, but either you entered the information wrong or you weren't born in Rochester, New York." What? Did I enter a wrong birth date? I have two sons also born in the month of May...did I perhaps type in their birth dates instead of mine? Surely I didn't have the wrong city name my whole life? Was I born in a different city that also began with an R?

I took a deep breath, and hit 8 on my cell phone. Reply to the call. Press 8, and hopefully find out I somehow randomly typed in a wrong bit of information on my application for a birth certificate copy.

"Rochester health records, how may I help you?"

I was fully awake by now, and made sure I was keenly aware of the dates and names that I was giving the clerk. May 18, 1966. The birth date I have celebrated ever since I could remember. The city: Rochester, NY. Please let this be a simple mistake. I've got a cruise to Mexico I need to enjoy.

"Give me just a few moments, and I'll run your information again."

Wait.

Wait.

Wait.

"I'm sorry, Mrs. Hart, I don't know what to say. We don't have any records on file for you."

"What do you suggest I do now?"

"You may want to contact the state records department in Albany. They should have your records. You may also want to try reordering your information on the birth certificate website. Sorry."

There it was. The call. The beginning of my new life journey. God was opening a door that I never knew existed. Deep breath.

Now what?

I called the Albany, NY state capitol's health records department. It took me a few operator transfers to finally get to the right office. As soon as I stated my situation, the kind woman let me know that their office wasn't able to give any information over the phone. I proceeded to let her know that I just wanted to know *if* my original copy of my birth certificate was at least in their files somewhere.

"I'm sorry, I'm not allowed to give any information over the phone. It all needs to be done through written correspondence."

"Please? I have to have a copy for a new passport, and I don't know what else to do."

Pause.

Pause.

"I'm not supposed to do this...but if you'll give me just a few minutes, I'll run your name through the system." Yes.

Wait.

Wait.

Elevator music.

Wait.

"I'm sorry, Mrs. Hart, we don't have any records on file for you." Pause. "Have you checked with the Adoption Registry Department?"

Shock.

Breathe.

Breathe.

Next thing I knew, I was being transferred to the Adoption Registry Department. Unreal.

The Adoption Registry lady wasn't very happy that the operator had transferred my call to her desk. She questioned who had transferred me, and being the shocked woman that I was, I hadn't thought to ask the first office lady her name.

"You should not have been transferred to this office."

"I'm sorry, but I have been trying every way I know to obtain a copy of my birth certificate, and I'm not really sure why I was transferred to you. Is there a possibility that my birth records would be in your office?"

"I can't tell you anything over the phone. Sorry." Click.

Forty-one. Forty-one years old, and sent to an Adoption Registry office. Unreal. I didn't have my birth certificate, but I can tell you what I DID have: a whole boat load of questions.

Chapter Two

With dead ends from the state of New York, I wondered what my next step should be, so I called my parents. I got the answering machine (yes they still have one of those) and left a message.

"Hi mom and dad, it's me. I am trying to get a copy of my birth certificate. I ordered one online, and when someone from Rochester contacted me back, she said they didn't have any records for me. I also got in touch with the state capitol, and they said they didn't have any records for me there, either. Do I have the wrong city name for where I was born? It is Rochester, yes? I'm second guessing myself, and it's kinda weird. Call me, OK?"
Five days passed. No return call.

After five days, I decided to give the parents a call myself. My dad answered, and started a conversation about the current weather across the nation. Really? I had left a message saying that my birth certificate couldn't be found *anywhere*, and I get a conversation about weather? If my child had called about the state saying they didn't have any documents about his birth, I would have already been on the phone to the state capitol and had those documents tracked down myself.

I finally ventured forth and asked if he had received my message about being born in Rochester or not. He assured me that indeed, I had been born in Rochester. When I informed him that neither Rochester nor Albany had any records for me, he suggested that possibly when my records were transferred over to microfiche, something had happened to my birth certificate. He then told me that he and my mom had kept my original birth certificate, and that they could send it to me in the mail.

The whole microfiche statement was strange. In this computer age, wouldn't documents be more readily accessible? I tried to put my questions aside, and anxiously awaited my original birth certificate to come in the mail.

A week later it came. When I opened the envelope to view my original birth certificate, I was a bit surprised. As a mom, I knew what my son's birth certificates looked like. As a wife, I had viewed Dave's certificate, but their documents looked totally different from the one I was holding in my hands. Odd, again. Odd seemed to be my new word.

This form that I held in my hands just said,

THIS IS TO VERIFY
That (my name)
BORN ON
May 18, 1966
IN THE CITY OF
Rochester, New York

It concluded with a signature and a stamped seal. That was it. No doctor's signature. No hospital name. No weight. No length. No witness signature. Nothing else.

I called my older brother. I only have one brother who is three years older than me. I wondered what his birth certificate looked like. I was starting to have some hunches. I told him that NY couldn't find any birth records for me, and he just laughed at what I was insinuating. "There's no way. You look and act just like mom, and I look more and more like dad every day."

I asked him if his birth certificate was nearby, and if he could get it. He did, and when we compared, we had the same exact form. Odd, again. He assured me that there was nothing to worry about, and that our different certificates must have just been what they handed out in New York during the 60's. Although he found my questions humorous, I couldn't help think of what so many kids tease their siblings about. "Mom and Dad adopted you." "Mom and Dad found you." "You're not related to anyone in the family." "The reason you look so different is because you were adopted." How 'hilarious' would it be if those comments actually applied to me or my brother. Or *both* of us?

Being a curious creature, I took my 'This Is To Verify' certificate to church that Sunday. I was going to get down to the bottom of my birth certificate dilemma. Surely in a church of our size, someone would be able to verify that they had a similar birth certificate. I was sure all of this was just a passing oddity, and life would get back to normal. Perhaps my original birth certificate really did get lost in a transfer. I look just like my mom...there's no way that I wasn't her daughter.

No one that I talked with at church had *ever* seen a certificate like mine. Great. Just great. I even found an ex-judge, and he wasn't sure what my document was. Finally I found an older woman who had lived in New York her whole life. She had even given birth to a child in New York around the same time that I was born.

Her child's certificate of live birth had the hospital, doctor, and oodles of other information on it. Mine had zilch, zero, nada, nothing.

Apparently my certificate wasn't what 'everyone' else had been handed for their official Certificate Of Live Birth in 1966.

Chapter Three

Nancy Drew. I had my new persona. I was the modern day Nancy Drew. I had a mystery sitting at my front door. I took the bait, and began to run. I was determined to find out why my 'original birth certificate' was so different. I love the internet. I began to search the exact wording of my birth certificate. I even looked up birth certificate forms issued in 1966. I spent hours searching and searching.

Everything that I came up with had the words 'falsified/amended birth certificate used for adoptions'. Nancy Drew was stunned. Perhaps I was a human example of what people say about dogs and their owners—after a while they begin to resemble each other. Did I really look like my mom because after forty-one years, I just *assumed* that I looked just like her? Was I really adopted? Was there someone else in the world that I looked like more? Adopted? What? A mystery waiting to be solved.

I still wasn't ready to give in to the fact that I had been adopted. I had so many clues pointing in that direction, but I just couldn't believe that my parents would keep something like that from me.

I wasn't twelve. I was a forty-one year-old mother of two teen age boys. I was an adult.

Who wouldn't tell their adult child that they were adopted? There just had to be another explanation. Perhaps if I could contact the hospital where I was born, they would be able to find my true original birth certificate. Perhaps in the dank, musty hospital basement, tucked deep in a hidden corner was a cabinet where my May 18, 1966 certificate was just waiting to be discovered. Perhaps.

I once again called my parent's home, and *once again* got the answering machine. Coincidence? I left a voice message asking my mom to call me with the name of the hospital where I was born. Nancy Drew would do the investigating once she had the name. Is it not sad that I didn't know the name of my birth hospital? Is that something that everyone else knows about themselves? So many questions.

Five days passed. Not a word. I didn't think they were on a trip? Why no answer?

On day six I called, and to my surprise, my mom answered.

"Hi, mom! Did you get my message? Could you possibly give me the name of the hospital where I was born? I'm hoping that perhaps I can trace my original birth certificate through that hospital."

"Well, I can't remember the name. It wasn't really a hospital, it was more like a clinic. Anyway, the building isn't there anymore. I think it burned down. The last time we visited Rochester, it wasn't there. You wouldn't be able to trace the records with the building gone."

"Well, do you at least remember what road it was on?"

"I think it may have been Monroe Road. Didn't the passport office accept your birth certificate that we sent you? I don't see what the problem is."

"Well, mom that form wasn't a Certificate of *Live* Birth. I want to find my copy of that. Its got to be somewhere."

"What we sent you was what we were handed. It's just what they handed out in those days. Don't be so worried. You have your certificate...everything is fine."

"Well, OK. Thanks, mom."

Stunned.

Just stunned.

What mother doesn't remember the name of the hospital where her child was born? Both of my boys were born at Hillcrest Medical Center in Tulsa, Oklahoma. Does a mother really forget that information? Furthermore, the *county* where I was born in was Monroe. Did that name just jump into her head because it was Monroe County? Did she make that up for the name of the street? I know that my mom had a serious operation in her late twenties, and I was born when she was thirty-two. With that operation, surely she would have to be in one of the best hospitals because of her previous medical condition.

Is my mother starting to lose her memory? She seems to remember everything else? I don't think she's going senile? Is it me? Am I just imagining all of this weirdness? What if my birth document really is the original, and I'm just overly curious for no reason. Have I jumped in the middle of a 1970's Scooby Doo cartoon, and am over thinking everything?

A few hours later, after processing the whole non-name of a hospital situation, I decided to call my mom again. I had to know. Was I adopted or not? Was there actually a reason for all this strangeness?

I made the call, and again, my mom answered the phone. I let her know that the records office sent me to the Adoption Registry office after telling me they had no records on file. I asked her if there was ANY reason why they should have done that. Answer: no. I asked her if there was ANYTHING she needed to tell me about all of this. Answer: no. I asked her if there would be ANY surprise that I might find out from the state of New York. Answer: no.

She asked me why I was so curious about all of this. (How could I *not* be curious?) She did everything to reassure me that indeed they *were* my parents, and that surely my forms had been lost or misplaced. I never came out and said the actual words, "Am I adopted?" If I wasn't adopted, that would have been a horrible thing to say to my parents. I gave her every chance in the world to admit that I was not her birth child. The last thing she said to me on the phone was, "If you have any questions, just look at my baby picture and your baby picture. We looked exactly alike."

So, once again, I took a question with me to church that Sunday. Was it normal for a woman to forget the name of the hospital where her child was born? Did I just assume that this was a common fact to remember? Well, I approached a large variety of women at church that day. All the young moms remembered as well as *all* the more 'seasoned' mothers. Every single mother remembered the name of the hospital where they gave birth. Every. Single. One. Just great...my mother was the only woman I knew who forgot the hospital name.

I took a giant step after that Sunday. It's a step I never dared to take, or believed I would ever take in my life. I questioned the words of truth my mom and dad told me. Questioning if your parents are telling you the truth is a very foreign place for me to go. I have just always assumed that parents never lied. Parents would tell you the truth no matter what.

I've always been a good girl. Obedient. Wanting to please. Never wanting to do any action against what my parents desired. I was about to cross into foreign territory. What good Christian girl doubts her parents? Is this territory into which I should even venture forth?

I love the Bible story of Elijah when Jezebel was after him. Elijah had just defeated the prophets of Baal on Mt. Carmel. Elijah laid down under a bush and asked to die. An angel fed him twice, and then he went off into the wilderness, and found a cave to hide in. The Word of the Lord told Elijah that Lord would be passing by.

"Then a great and powerful wind tore the mountains apart and shattered the rocks before the LORD, but the LORD was not in the wind. After the wind there was an earthquake, but the LORD was not in the earthquake. After the earthquake came a fire, but the LORD was not in the fire. And after the fire came a gentle whisper. When Elijah heard it, he pulled his cloak over his face and went out and stood at the mouth of the cave."
Isaiah 19:12-13.

I've never heard a loud audible booming voice of God, but I have heard whispers in my heart. Sometimes it's so easy to think that the voice is just in our head, or that we're making up the thoughts or words we're hearing.

I do believe with all my heart that God was whispering to me "...*find out more*...". I had to cross over into unknown territory. I'm so thankful that my amazing husband was supportive of every move I made. He encouraged me to trust my heart, and that still small voice. God was beginning to unveil my story. A story He had waited forty-one years to reveal.

Chapter Four

So I had this mystery in my lap. Unanswered questions and missing puzzle pieces swirled in my head. What to do with all of this? As I continued to hear God's still small voice whispering to me "*...find out more...*" I debated as to what my next step should be. I felt I had run into a dead end information-wise from my parents. That cow was milked dry. It was time to leap out in faith. Time to take a giant step into uncharted territory. It was time to contact the New York Adoption Registry Office.

I'm not much of a secret keeper. Don't get me wrong, if you tell me something in confidence not to share with others, I'm solid. You can rely on me. In elementary school I could keep a 'crush' secret. No problem. Other than a few instances in college (shhh) I've *never* kept anything from my parents. I enjoy sharing with them the details of my life. I'm pretty much an open book with my mom and dad. This was different. I was journeying out on my own. This I had to do for myself. This was to be *my* new secret.

I called the Adoption Registry office. It was a little embarrassing to share with them that I didn't really know (at age forty-one) if I had been adopted or not. What was my next step in finding out if I had adoption papers in their office, I asked. They informed me that I needed to download the Adoption Registry application. Send that in, and then they would process the papers, and be in touch with me. They let me know that I would never receive the actual name of my birth parents, but that they would send me what they called non-identifying information. Dates, ages, race, time of birth, etc., but nothing that would identify who my actual birth mother was.

It seemed simple yet mind-boggling at the same time. Who doesn't know that they're adopted? Who goes forty-one years of their life without one *clue* of adoption? All my life I heard how I looked *just* like my mom. How I *sang* just like my mom. How many times had I heard that cute little saying "That apple sure doesn't fall far from the tree"? I was beginning to question if I actually wasn't an apple. Perhaps I was an orange grown in a completely different state. What if I came from a *grove* instead of an *orchard? What if, what if, what if?*

I've watched enough news documentary shows throughout the years to hear stories of adopted children. So many have said, "I always felt different. I didn't feel like I fit." Total opposite with me. Seriously, in forty-one years of life in my family, I *never* felt like I didn't belong. I looked just like my mom. My brother looked like my dad.

My parents were musically inclined and gifted. Music just came naturally to me, and felt like second nature. I've been singing since my earliest memories, and have played the cello since fourth grade. My creative side mirrored my parents perfectly. No doubts ever that I wasn't their flesh and blood. Until that phone call.

I never once heard a relative say a comment that would make me think 'that was odd...?' No one ever made me feel or believe that I wasn't one hundred percent a full-blooded relative. I am grateful for that, but at the same time it makes me wonder if *they* knew if I was adopted or not? Did my parents adopt me and keep it a secret from *everyone* on both sides of the family? Did my mom fake my pregnancy? Would she really do a thing like that? *Surely* not.

There were four pages full of information that I needed to fill out to be accepted into the Adoption Registry. I had enough information for a quarter of one of those pages. Seriously. I had my name, my parents names, my city of birth (hoping that I at least had *that* information correct) and my birth date. That was it. The other forms needed information about the official date of adoption. Nothing. Do you have information about the hospital where you were born? Nothing. Any other known birth siblings? Nothing. Time of birth? Nothing. Weight, length? Nothing, nothing. Adoption agency used? Nothing. Official adoption documents? Nothing. I was reliving nightmares of taking a high school exam, and knowing *none* of the answers, other than my name at the top of the page.

I prepared the forms, got them notarized, and sent off to Albany, New York. Now to wait.

I could just imagine all the office girls at the Adoption Registry when they opened up my packet. "Hey girls...ya gotta read *this* one. Forty-one year-old woman doesn't have a clue if she's adopted or not. Hardly has any information written. Poor thing. This is one for the record books. And she lives in Houston, Texas. She went from New York to Houston? Bet they at least have some good Mexican food down there. All right...now who wants to process *this* one? "

Two weeks after sending off my packet, I received an official looking letter back from the Adoption Registry office. Here it was. The letter I had been anticipating. My answer was waiting to be read. This letter could change both my past and my future at the same moment. My truth had simply been typed onto a piece of paper, folded into an envelope, and sent to my mailbox. So simple yet so utterly complex. What if I found out that my parents really *were* my biological parents? All this craziness for nothing.

Deep breath.

Open carefully.

Don't rip the letter.

Sit down.

"Dear Mrs. Hart,
We have accepted your application into the Adoption Registry of New York. As soon as we have any information for you, we will get it to you. Please know that this could take a minimum of 6-12 months. We will do our best.
Thank you."

Short and simple. Perhaps a tad too simple. No definite answers. I thought for sure that this letter was official proof that I had been adopted. Dave was siding towards a more conservative approach, "What if this just means that they have accepted your application, but that they are still needing to *check* to see *if* you have an adoption file in the Adoption Registry Office?"

Great.

Back to ground zero.

Why couldn't they have just said, "Yes, you were adopted, and yes we have your official Certificate of Live Birth and your adoption papers in our *hands* and *in* our office." Would that have been too much to ask? "...*find out more*..."

OK, God. I'm trying to find out, but it's not an easy process. No definites. Now I have to wait six to twelve months. How do I do that?

"Those that wait upon the Lord shall renew their strength,
they shall mount up with wings as eagles.
They shall run and not be weary,
They shall walk and not faint.
Teach me Lord,
Teach me Lord
To wait..."

September rolled into October. Fall was in the air. Mums were planted. Pansies were added to the outside flower beds. Giant Pixi Stix were handed out to the neighborhood trick-or-treaters. Pumpkin candles were bought and burned. Turkey, mashed potatoes, green bean casserole, and pumpkin pie was devoured and enjoyed. Jackets were dug out from the back of the closet. The heat was turned on. The fireplace swept out and ready. (Yes, even in Houston!)

The tree was decorated beautifully. Homemade ornaments from our first year of marriage intermingled with those darling Sunday School ornaments carefully sculpted by our sons over the years. Turkey (or was it ham?) was enjoyed along with cranberry fluff and a kitchen full of additional side dishes. Christmas carols were sung at church, presents were opened. We rang in the New Year, and still no word from the Adoption Registry office.

A new year.

New possibilities.

Old unanswered questions still lingered.

Was I adopted?

Chapter Five

Scenarios scenarios scenarios. Oh my, the scenarios that were floating through my head. The first scenario was that this journey of questioning was for nothing. I would find out from the Adoption Registry that my parents were in fact my birth parents. My imagination had run overtime, and everything in life was as it had been for forty-one years. My brother was my brother. We both came out of the same womb. All normal. I looked like my mom for a reason, because birth daughters carry the same DNA as their parents. All. Just. Normal.

The adoption scenarios had a mind of their own. The endless possibilities took me out of everyday life to the land of 'Wonder Who'. Wonder Who gave me up for adoption. Wonder Who she was. Wonder Who was my birth father. Wonder if they married. Wonder if they're still alive. Wonder if I have siblings. Wonder if they've tried to search for me. Wonder if they care. Wonder if they remember.

Perhaps my birth mother had been a singer on Broadway. My birth father, a European Aristocrat who fell madly and passionately in love with this 'Woman of the Theater'. His family would never approve of her. She didn't come from the same high-brow breeding and money, but that didn't keep them apart.

Keeping their forbidden romance a secret, they found themselves torn between two worlds. The desires of the heart conflicting with the demands of high society. Their wonton love created a child. A child they could never keep, but so desperately desired. A child that would forever be proof that *love,* above *all* else triumphs.

After keeping the pregnancy a secret for as long as she could, the Broadway singer heart-brokenly decided to journey upstate, and find an Adoption Agency that would lovingly place this permanent symbol of a life she could never have in someone else's arms. But one day. One day when she finally had her name in lights, she would search for that child. She would make that baby girl hers forever.

Dave, on the other hand presented a completely different prospective birth mother story. He suggested that the circus had come through town that Spring. The Freak Circus to be exact. The Fat Bearded Lady had a wild fling with the Sword Swallower. She had no idea she was pregnant all of the nine months. One night in May, she thought she perhaps had food poisoning, and went to lay down. I popped out. *Shock.* She stuck me in a cardboard box, and placed me on the steps of the Rochester Adoption Agency. The end.

I liked mine better.

My 'friends' weren't much better, either. Some started calling me Baby Moses. Funny, huh. Perhaps I had been born, placed in a basket, and floated down a river. Those funny friends of mine, they're such encouragers.

I couldn't leave out the cheerleader option. Perhaps she was an adorable seventeen year-old cheerleader at Rochester High School. The sweetest of the squad, and a member of the First Methodist youth group. An all-around great girl. A friend to both the popular *and* unpopular crowd. Her only flaw was falling in love with the handsome star football player. Every girl dreamed of being his. My birth mother *was* his.

It was their senior year of high school. Such a bright future lay waiting for both of them. With their pedigrees, they could enter any Ivy League college they chose. The future was set. It was promising. It was destined.

The Homecoming Game was a triumph. Electricity filled the air. The world was theirs. Their romance budded into passion that night. A first for both. Awkward, yet everything they dreamed it would be. How could something wrong feel so right?

Two months later, fear gripped the her heart. It couldn't be. No. No. *Noooo.*

The beautiful cheerleader secretly and suddenly slipped out of society. Hidden. Word around school was that she went to live with, and help out an elderly aunt in Indiana. She would stay with her through the summer, and then be off to college.

She was never in Indiana. She was in a girl's home in downtown Rochester, NY. She was put out of sight with all the other girls in town that were no longer so innocent, and no longer accepted. Nine months later, she had a baby girl. That was 1966.

———————————

It's crazy, isn't it? To have no idea of where you came from? To not know what your nationality is? Who your people are? To sit and wonder and dream through scenario after scenario?

It was time. I had to know. Yes or no. Adopted. Not adopted.

I dug in my desk drawer, and found a little note card and envelope. I didn't need a large piece of paper. The note card was the perfect size.

"I have sent in my Adoption Registry forms. I still have no idea if I was adopted or not. Could you please verify for me in writing whether or not I do indeed have a sealed adoption file in your office.

Thank you."

Sometimes simple is best. That's what I needed to know. That's what I asked for. Stamp. Mail. Wait.

Three weeks later the mailman delivered it. A simple white envelope. A New York address in the upper left hand corner. My name and 13123 Finch Brook Drive in the middle. Here it was. Hopefully a definite answer. All these months of waiting. It would be in black letters on a white piece of paper. My revealed past and future destiny all rolled up into one answer. Was I ready? This could change everything.

"...find out more..."

Gentle with the envelope.

Deep breath.

This is what you've been waiting for.

Steady.

"Dear Ms. Hart:

This is in response to your January 22, 2008, letter.

The Adoption Registry has verified that you were born and adopted in New York State. We are now in the process of obtaining available information about your birth parents and your adoption from the court that finalized the adoption. If the court indicates that an agency was involved in the adoption, we will contact the agency as well for information.

Please be assured that we will contact you as soon as we have obtained available information.

Sincerely,

Peter M. Carucci
Director"

My answer was staring at me, and I stared back. I felt numbness, shock, disbelief, confusion, and yet a strange sensation of excitement all at once. How does one *ever* prepare for this kind of information? I found out I'm adopted through a *letter*. A *letter*.

My hunches had been right. There was a little self satisfaction with that thought. I wasn't crazy after all. I hadn't been imagining that there was something strange going on. I'm adopted. I'm *adopted*. Adopted? *Adopted.*

I read and re-read that letter. It was just a simple short letter, but I wanted to soak up every word of truth that had been revealed to me. That word was now who I was. *Adopted.* Someone out there other than the parents that raised me gave birth to me. I'm not half Russian, a quarter Scottish and a quarter Irish. Wonder what nationality I am? I bet I'm Italian. I *talk* with my hands a lot. In fact, I have a hard time talking *without* my hands. Yes. I think I must be Italian. I love garlic bread. I'm a huge manicotti fan. I'm sure it's in my blood. I wonder if I'm full-blooded Italian, or do I have some other nationality mixed in?

My parents. My parents *never* told me. Why in the world not? Why? Granted, I never came out and directly asked, "Am I adopted" with the phone calls over the summer, but still. My mom *knew* what I was insinuating when I questioned her. *Why?* Why didn't she tell me the truth?

My brother. I must call him. See, I was right. Told you so. My brother was the first person I called. I never dreamed I would be calling him with this kind of information I read him the letter, and he was speechless. At least I knew for sure that *I* was adopted. I didn't have any proof of his adoption. Perhaps he *was* their biological son. What if we weren't even related at *all*.

Leaving my brother confused and stunned, I encouraged him to do a little digging, and see what his story was. His brand new life story.

How many times can one read and re-read an impersonal, direct, and short letter? This one letter. Now what do I do? I had crossed over into new territory. I looked behind, and the bridge was destroyed—never to be crossed over again. Can't go back. "No turning back...No turning back". No longer did I have the identity which I had claimed for forty-one years. I was a new person.

I was an *adoptee.*

Don't get me wrong. By age forty-one I knew who I *was.* I knew my talents. I knew my role as wife and mother. I was confident in who I was in God's eyes. I knew my likes and dislikes. I knew my strengths and weaknesses. I just didn't know who I *was.* *Was* as in who I came from. Were there hereditary traits that I should have developed, but never did because of how I was raised? Could there be mental illness in my genetic make-up? Who *am* I really? What is in my DNA? Please, oh, please don't let me discover I really *did* come from the Freak Show Circus. Please.

I wouldn't be honest if I didn't admit that, despite the life-changing circumstances, I had a stirring of curious intrigue deep down. I was a *mystery.* I was at the precipice of an unknown discovery. Uncharted paths lay in waiting. Nancy Drew had just been handed the case of a lifetime.

Chapter Six

I had all this new information in my lap. The question that burned in my heart was how do I intertwine this discovery into my relationship with my parents? Plainly spoken...how in the world do I tell them I know?

The last thing I wanted to do was hurt my parents. I had been nothing but unconditionally loved my whole life. I still wanted to honor my parents, but I felt at this point I needed to let them know the information I had just received: although this was obviously information that they had known for forty-one years. Nothing necessarily new to them. The newness was the fact that now I knew the truth.

I grabbed a spiral college ruled notebook and pen. I started writing.

Mom and Dad,

If you're not sitting down right now, you may want to. Monday afternoon, February 11th, I received the letter from New York that is enclosed. Needless to say, it was kind of a shock. I'm guessing it is also quite a shock for you to see.

I have no anger in this letter. I don't know your reasoning in keeping this a secret. I thank you both for a wonderful childhood. I will be eternally grateful for your love, support, encouragement, gymnastics, ballet, tap, cello and voice lessons. I thank you for taking care of my needs and wants. I thank you for a free college education—and the list goes on. None of that will ever change.

I don't want our relationship and friendship to change, either. What I do desire is my story. How I came into your lives. If you know who my birth parents were, etc. Obviously I have a huge list of questions. Being forty-one, I would like to find out the health history of my birth parents, if that is available.

The State of New York's Adoption Registry will be able to provide me with non-identifying information about my birth parents. For example, I can find out their ages, education, job status, nationality, and a description of their physical appearance. I will try to locate them, if they are still alive. Again—any information that you might have would save me huge amounts of time and money.

I have a new chapter and journey in my life. My prayer is that you won't have any anger with this situation. I firmly believe that 'the steps of a righteous man are ordered of God'. I don't believe any of this is happening by accident. God already knows my future events.

I would like to go on this journey with both of you. It would be such a blessing to know how I came into your lives. You don't have to keep my adoption a secret anymore. That must be somewhat of a relief to you both.

You may respond to this letter however you choose. I welcome this next step in our relationship. You will forever be my parents, and my love for you will be constant.

Kirsten

I did it. I didn't think it was too harsh. It was time to get this out into the open. Seal. Stamp. Mail. Wait.

———————————

Now to begin with the search for my birth mother. Was she even still alive? 'Rejoice for the steps of a righteous man are ordered of God'. I had to trust that every step of this journey had been ordered of God. Preordained. Already planned. Already known. I just had to do my part unraveling the mystery. I had to use what God had given me. My brain, my heart, and my instincts. God could do the impossible, but I needed to do the footwork. He gave me the puzzle box: I just needed to dump all the pieces out, and start putting the picture together...piece by piece.

Where to start? I knew that I would be getting non-identifying information from the Adoption Registry. I also knew that information could take at the very least six months, if not longer. I didn't want to wait that long. Plus, I wouldn't have exact information. I was looking for a name. Hopefully the name of a woman who was still alive.

I could go through all of this searching, and find that the woman who gave me life was already passed on to another world. What if my birth mother had been searching for years, but gave up after forty-one years thinking that *I* was the one who didn't want to be found? '...*find out more*...' God had given me those words. I was was hoping that my whole search wouldn't lead to a dead end. Trust. Where could she be?

I had the internet. I had the world at my fingertips. Could the information I was so desperately searching for be within the world wide web? Was her name sitting in some obscure website just waiting to be found? Start with my birth date.

I put my birth date into the search box on my computer screen. I also added the words 'birth mother searching for daughter'. I scrambled my birth date, place of birth, my status as an adoptee, and every other clever wording I could think of umpteen times. My discovery? There were thousands upon thousands of people searching for lost family members. I had unlocked a whole new world. A sea of individuals on a quest for their own missing puzzle piece.

Since adoption had never touched my life before this season, I just didn't realize the magnitude of how adoption affected so many on all sides of the issue. I had friends that were adopted, and knew of families that had adopted children, but the vastness of individuals searching for one another astounded me.

Now I was just another teensy fish swimming through this world of lost birth family members.

Chapter Seven

During the beginning of my birth mother search, my husband and I took our second cruise that year. And yes, I just said *second*. The cruise that I needed the passport for, we took as a whole family in October. It was delightful except for having a horse in Mexico flip over twice and roll in the sand while I was still riding it. That's another story. A great and crazy story. I survived. Barely.

This *second* cruise we took during Valentine's Day week. We left our boys home for this one. Again, we were leading the singing, but had plenty of play time. Leaving our boys home during the seven days we were gone was a big step. They were very capable and reliable teenagers. Amazing teenagers. We had been out on sea three days when we docked in Cozumel, Mexico.

We had discovered a teensy glitch. We told the boys that we were to arrive back at port and be home on Friday. It wasn't until after we were in the the middle of the Gulf of Mexico that we realized that our Galveston arrival was Saturday instead of Friday. How awful would it be for our boys to expect us on Friday, and hear and see nothing. They had watched too many sinking ship

45

movies. It would not rest well for us to not return when expected. Since we didn't have cell phone coverage on the ship, I was anxious to find an internet cafe, and let our boys know of the change in arrival.

While everyone else was snorkeling and going on grand adventures, Dave and I found an alley with a $2.50 an hour internet establishment.

Before I composed my email to our guys, I surveyed my inbox emails. One email address quickly caught my attention. My heart skipped a beat. The email was sent from the Adoption Registry office. Could my information be in this email? Was I ready?

I opened the email, and started to read. Yes, indeed they had details for me. No name, but new knowledge.

Birth mother age at birth: 24

Time of birth: 1:00 am

Inches: 21 ½

Weight: 6 lb. 5 oz.

Delivered at 42 weeks.

Previous children: No

No birth father was listed on the birth records.

Birth mother nationality: German

As soon as we find the Adoption Agency used in the adoption, we will get their information to you.

There it was. My first morning rays of insight. Minimal to some— a treasure chest to me. I read, read, and then re-read those tidbits of my identity. Birth mother age: twenty-four. My Harlequin Romance for Young Reader's cheerleader and football captain novel was now nullified. At least I hoped so. How sad would it be to have a birth mother at age twenty-four still on the high school cheer squad. The up and coming Broadway singer/actress scenario suddenly took prime positioning. Twenty-four. Not seventeen. She was probably out of college. *If* she had gone to college.

There was something comforting about knowing what time I had been born. My first son had been born at 12:46 am. Just a fourteen minute difference from my own birth time. It is a peaceful time at night. Subdued lighting. Peace amidst the pain. I wonder if the atmosphere in my birth mother's room was peaceful when she delivered me? Was her heart at peace? *Peace.* A twenty-four year old girl becoming a woman in her own right, while tormented by the agony of giving her baby away. *Her* baby. *I* was *her* baby.

Six pounds and five ounces is a small baby, and I was two weeks late. Interesting. Ryan, my youngest was also born two weeks past his birth date. I wonder if late deliveries is genetic. *Is* that something that could be genetic? Interesting. Six pounds and five ounces at forty-two weeks. I wonder what my birth weight would have been if I had been born on my due date. That's pretty small. I wonder if I'm just way off the charts for my current poundage, and what my body frame naturally should be holding weight wise. I need to lose some weight.

No birth father listed. *No birth father listed.* That makes me a
_____. My mom always taught me that the 'b' word was
a bad word. Now it's who I *am.* I am a bastard baby. Kirsten Hart
Bastard Baby. Illegitimate sounds so much kinder. No. Bastard. I
can't believe I'm saying that word. The 'b' word. Laugh or cry. Is it
odd to find humor in this? All my life I had not a clue that I was
adopted much less an illegitimately born bastard child. The 'b'
word would no longer be known as a bad word in our household.
It was an identity word. My identity word. My *previous* identity.
"...Behold, I make all things new..."

God knew who I was and where I came from. He knew the
moment I was conceived. He is at the same time the past,
present, *and* future. He knew the title of my birth rank, yet at
the same time knew who I would *become.* All things new. *All.* A
bastard-born baby into a Child of God. No inheritance to full birth
right. Beauty from ashes.

For the duration of my internet session, I felt as though I had
melted into another reality. Here I was on one of the most
beautiful Caribbean islands with the sounds and smells of
tropical paradise muffled by the reality of my new truth.

"Your session is up in five minutes, ma'am".

The words bolted me back to the present. The boys. I had to let
the boys know about returning on Saturday. I sent my email off
to my guys. Let them know we were doing great, and informed
them of our change in arrival. Kisses and love, Mom. *Mom.* At
least I knew *that* much about myself. I was a mom with two
precious boys. I was also a wife. I was a wife, and my husband
and I were on a breathtaking *island.* It was time to enjoy this slice

of utopia.

On the ship later that evening as we headed out to our next port of call, story lines swirled on sheets of imaginary paper. What was the script of this young twenty-four year old German woman? Who was my nameless mystery birth father. What was *his* story? I tried to maintain my sea legs, but the weight of my unknown tale wove its way through my rubbery appendages. It was time to go on deck, find a chaise lounge, and reflect. Peace on the lido deck. Sweet moonlit peace.

Chapter Eight

Soon after arriving back home, my search took off. I shook the sand off my flip-flops, and put on my detective cap. Full steam ahead.

I happened upon a few sites that were registries set up for birth mothers to connect with their children. The websites were relatively new, but the registries themselves had been in existence for years. I entered my birth date and information into both registries. The information provided for me stated that if there was a match, they would get in touch with me via email. I had time. I could wait for my email. Could it be that simple? Yes, it could be. If my birth mother had registered her information to find me, I would receive an email with her information. That easy. Easy.

I waited, and heard nothing. That dreaded 'what if' thought struck again. What if I never find her? What if she's not alive?

The next week yielded a unique discovery. From my hours upon hours of searching, I discovered a chat group on www.yahoo.com. This chat group consisted of New York only adoptees and birth mothers searching for each other. That narrowed my search tremendously. That was a good thing.

Viewing through this site, I deciphered that the proper etiquette to joining this group was to add your story, and give details of who you were searching for.

Hi Everyone,

I am just starting out on my quest to find my birth parents. On Monday, February the 11th, I received and official statement from the Adoption Registry in NY that verified that I had been both born AND adopted in New York. This past summer I was searching for my birth certificate for a new passport, and couldn't find it. I tried to order one through vitalcheck, and got a phone call that they didn't have any information for me. That started my quest.

Both my parents have denied the adoption. It has been eight and a half months since I asked them questions. I sent my application to the Adoption Registry, but still wasn't really sure that I had sealed adoption records...until this past Monday. It is unreal...but yet I know there is a reason this is happening in my life. Of course, to be reunited with both of my birth parents (and possible siblings) would be an answer to prayer.

Who has my eyes..hands...laugh...smile? So many questions.

I look forward to this journey, and the support of this group.

Kirsten Hart

There it was in a nutshell. My life. My new life story. Out in public for the first time.

It didn't take long for responses. These were helpful and supportive people. I was now one of them. A person searching for the truth. Searching for a name. Searching for an identity. Searching for long-lost answers. I had found a new place of comfort. I could be honest with these individuals. They one-hundred percent understood my story, and what I was feeling down deep. I liked them.

There were so many encouraging messages to my initial posting. I learned a new term: Search Angels. Search Angels were mostly women who volunteered their time and energy to help in the search process, many of whom had searched for answers themselves. New registries, contacts, and valuable search tips were emailed to me. "Rejoice for the *steps* of a righteous man are ordered of God". Thank you God for revealing these new steps in which to walk. I was trusting that each step I was taking was heading me in the right direction. The direction of leading me to the truth of who I was.

There were quite a number of adoptees from Rochester. One gentleman wrote to me sharing his personal journey. He, too, was adopted to a family in Rochester. He was also born in 1966, and told me about the three different adoption agencies that were active that year. He had been adopted from the North Haven Agency, also known as the Rochester Maternal and Adoption Service. He told me if I had been adopted through this agency, that I could get all kinds of information from them. Very interesting.

I decided to do a little research myself. Perhaps it *could* be this easy. What in the world kind of place was I adopted from? I looked up the adoption agency name on the internet. The information I found was a tad shocking.

'In 1905, the Rochester Orphan Asylum moved to a 30-acre location on Pinnacle Hill (what is now the Monroe Avenue headquarters of Hillside Family of Agencies). The new location was built as an innovative cottage system to reflect the changing theories in caring for children. Efforts were focused on keeping troubled children within the parental home or family unit, with the entire family receiving necessary services. When a family's situation made this impossible, the child would be removed from the home and housed in an institution. At the Rochester Orphan Asylum, the cottages created a home-like environment within the boundaries of the institution.

To reflect the shift from providing a home for orphans to caring for "dependent and neglected children," the Rochester Orphan Asylum changed its name in 1921 to Hillside Home for Children. Another name change came in 1940 when Hillside Children's Center was adopted and a goal set: "for every child, a fair chance for the development of a healthy personality."'

All this was so unbelievable. Unbelievable that the history above contained the words: unfortunate, erring, and transient. *Transient.* That word made me stomach churn. What if that is who I am? Just an unwanted baby from a *transient* girl. An unfortunate and *erring* German transient girl.

54

I read and re-read the history of the Rochester Community Home for Girls which eventually became The Hillside Children's Center. It was time to check with them to see if I, in fact, came from someone that had been a part of this institution.

I looked up the phone number, and called. After once again sharing how I discovered that I had been adopted, the very kind woman sitting in Rochester, New York let me know that she would do some checking and get back with me in a few days. I was getting closer. I could feel it.

The other two agencies I contacted didn't have my information registered. I had all my eggs in one basket at this point. One adoption agency basket.

The call came. I heard the word yes. Yes, I had been adopted through their agency. Yes, they had papers from my adoption. Yes, I would be receiving information about my birth mother. No name, but pages of information. *Pages.* Nancy Drew was closing in.

Chapter Nine

Are You My Mother? Written and illustrated by P.D. Eastman, the children's book *Are You My Mother?* relates the story of a young bird's search for his mother, who had left the nest to find food for her new infant a few moments before he hatched. It's an adorable book I used to read to my boys when they were little. Baby Bird, who is too young to fly, leaves the nest and conducts his search on foot. In a bizarre twist of fate, he walks right by his mother without ever seeing her, as she pulls the worm destined to be his breakfast from the ground.

"I did have a mother," said the baby bird. "I know I did. I have to find her. I will. I WILL!"

Armed with only his innate curiosity and strong resolve, Baby Bird interrogates the strangers he meets on the way, but neither the kitten nor the hen, the dog, the cow, the old car, the tugboat, or the airplane respond to his oft-repeated question positively. In what is clearly the climactic scene in the story, Baby Bird sees a big thing (a steam shovel):

"There she is!" he said. "There is my mother!" He ran right up to it. "Mother, Mother! Here I am, Mother!" he said to the big thing.

As anyone who read this story or had it read to them as a child probably remembers, the big thing just said, **"SNORT."**

The big thing deposits Baby Bird back in his nest, just as Mother Bird returns to the nest with the worm. Mother and son are joyously reunited.

I *was* Baby Bird. I was on an endless quest to find my long lost mother. Where *was* she? I wanted my joyous reunion, too.

———————————

My search kept leading me to the name Lorraine Dusky. I discovered an article that she had written years ago. The words piqued my interest: "If you knew me when my daughter was born, in 1966 in Rochester N.Y., you might guess I would be one of them today: a birth mother who was supposed to 'get on' with her life. The father, a married man with a public life, had to be "protected". For his sake, and yes mine, I operated in deepest secrecy. A catholic girl, a year out of college, so deep was my shame that I hid my pregnancy from my family in another state."

I was intrigued. Could this be my birth mother? A year out of college would have put her at the exact age that my report had stated. A 'married man with a public life' logically explained why there had not been a birth father listed on my papers. Catholic? I suppose there were some German Catholics. Could it be this easy? Was my birth mother reaching out to me through her

58

articles?

I dug deeper. I researched more of her writings. Every word seemed to draw me closer. Ms. Dusky had written a book in the early 1980's, I read, that was titled 'Birthmark'. Scanning the back cover review, my heart waned as I viewed the words in front of me. In 1981, she had hired a private investigator to locate her daughter, and they were reunited months later. So close. I couldn't get over the fact that she had been in Rochester the same time that my birth mother was there. Was there any chance that in that small world of young women giving their children up for adoption, that perhaps, she may have known my birth mother? They would have been the same age. A shot in the dark, but my only lead at that point.

Nancy Drew put her investigating cap and cloak on. I would locate Lorraine Dusky. Could she have my missing puzzle piece? Was she holding the clue to break open the case? Would she remember another twenty-three year-old college graduate in Rochester, New York that had walked through the same heartbreak as she? What were the chances? Two twenty-three year old girls. Two baby girls born in May 1966. One found. One searching. Only time and a phone call would tell.

Once again, the internet was my friend. It didn't take too long to locate a Lorraine Dusky who lived on Long Island, New York. By now I knew she was a woman's rights activist, author, and newspaper reporter. What I didn't know was how she would respond to an out of the blue call from someone wanting information from 1966.

I called. She answered. After a few introductory questions to see if I had the *right* Lorraine Dusky, we started a wonderful conversation about life back in Rochester, New York. I liked her. I kind of wished she were my birth mother. We conversed about the home for unwed mothers, and I asked if she remembered another young mother to be that had been her same age. No recollection. Disappointment.

She did ask a poignant question. "Aren't you angry with your parents for not telling you you were adopted?" I was rather surprised at my quick response, "no". The words that followed were, "I'm not angry. I'm disappointed, but I don't feel anger. I'm disappointed and confused as to why they felt they had to keep this secret from me." I then went on to add, "It's actually kind of exciting. Exciting to know I have a birth mother out in the world somewhere, and possibly other siblings. I know that may sound odd, but I'm excited about what my future holds."

I really did feel that way. My husband and I had already walked through a time in our lives of holding anger towards a family member. Years before. Thought we'd hold this family member accountable for their actions, and wanted them to feel the disappointment we felt. It, in particular, weighed heavily on my husband. The hurt and anger was affecting his health, and it was almost literally eating him up from the inside out.

During that time, we were asked to sing for a revival at a sweet country church in Oklahoma. We did our part, and sat down to hear the message. The whole message was on forgiveness. When the preacher quoted the Bible verse Matthew 6:15. "If you do not forgive men their sins, your Father will not forgive your sins." Yikes. That was a serious eye-opener. We sure didn't want to be living in unforgiveness. Unforgiveness of others or ourselves. Letting go of the anger and frustration was so freeing. We walked away from that Oklahoma country church with a fresh understanding of how forgiveness could be so freeing to the soul and mind. Lesson learned. Preparation for the journey with my adopted parents.

Lorraine and I chatted more, and she ended the conversation with letting me know that if I ever needed to talk about anything, she was there for me. Great woman. Although we had an enjoyable time of getting to know each other, I still wasn't any closer to finding my actual birth mother. Journey onward.

The phone call with Lorraine Dusky got me thinking about my relationship with my parents. Would it ever be the same again? What would they say to me? What do I say to them? I still was in shock to think that they had kept this a secret for forty-one years. I wonder if there were times when they wanted to tell me. Did they feel they missed the perfect timing, and then just decided to keep quiet about it for the rest of my life? Did they really think that I would just turn my back on them and desert them as parents? After forty-one years of being their child, did they not trust my love and our relationship together? No, I didn't feel anger, but I had a lot of questions that needed answers.

Chapter Ten

In shady, green pastures, so rich and so sweet,
God leads His dear children along;
Where the water's cool flow bathes the weary one's feet,
God leads His dear children along.

Some through the waters, some through the flood,
Some through the fire, but all through the blood;
Some through great sorrow, but God gives a song,
In the night season and all the day long.

Sometimes on the mount where the sun shines so bright,
God leads His dear children along;
Sometimes in the valley, in darkest of night,
God leads His dear children along.

Thank you George A. Young for penning such beautiful and comforting words. God. Leads. Us. Along. An old hymn with a timeless message. I wasn't necessarily in my 'darkest of night'.

My children and husband were healthy. If they weren't, that would be *my* darkest of night. I did feel, though, that God was definitely leading me along. Leading me along a new path of discovery, and understanding.

Weeks had gone by without a word from my parents. If I could have only been a fly on their wall. The unknown is what plays with your mind. Were they just on a very long trip that they never told me about? Were they scared? Upset? No answers. Of course, I could have called them, but I felt I had done my part. I had sent the letter. I had just found out that I *wasn't* their biological daughter. They had known this my whole life. I was the one in shock with this unknown detail. I was ready for my mom and dad to be the ones to make the next move and contact me. Weeks continued to pass. Nothing.

The chorus of God Leads Us has the words, 'but God gives a song'. Being a Worship Pastor's wife, my everyday is filled with Christian music. I grew up a Minister of Music's daughter, and I ended up marrying someone in the same field. I have been surrounded by inspirational music my whole life. It has always interested me how the human mind can remember lyrics to thousands of songs. It's easier for me to remember words when they're put to music.

Suddenly the lyrics to so many songs that I had sung throughout my life seemed instantly relevant. I'd find myself singing songs just walking through the house...or doing dishes, or laundry. God really *did* give me a song after song after song. Verses and the chorus of It Is Well would flow. My spirit would lift when I'd sing along to CD's in the car. A dear friend of mine is Alvin Slaughter. I'd pop in his CD's, and instantly I would feel renewed. One of Alvin's songs: ANYTHING, has the following lyrics:

God can do anything
Anything and everything
There ain't nothing He cannot do
God can do anything
Anything and everything
He can do everything but fail

I believed those words as I sang them over and over. In my best female black gospel (car only) voice, I'd belt those lyrics. Whatever doors were shut in my finding my birth mother 'There ain't *nothing* He cannot do'. I held those words so close to my heart. I can't count the number of times I'd listen, sing along, and hit the rewind button. Songs, and scripture put to songs carried me through.

Some through great sorrow, but God gives a song,
In the night season and all the day long.

While I was patiently waiting for my report from the adoption agency, I read something that caught my interest on the yahoo adoptees chat group site. A woman posted that she had been searching for her birth mother for over twenty-five years, hired a search company, and they located her in three weeks. Impressive. The next week another woman posted that after years and years of searching, she had hired the same company, and they had located her birth mother in four weeks. Impressive, again.

In the following days, I read their postings of contact made with their birth moms, and was able to experience their reunions alongside of them, so to speak. I didn't know if I had twenty years to search. Time was of the essence to me, so I took a giant (mother may I?) step forward. I contacted both of these women for the information on the search agency they used. It only took a few hours for a response. I had a name. I searched the agency, and got all the contact information. I made the call. The voice on the other end asked who I was searching for, and what information I had already attained. "All I have", I told them "Is my name, birth date, parents names, and the name of the adoption agency." I didn't get a very positive response.

The company let me know that NY is an extremely closed state when it came to adoption records. The records were sealed, they told me. Many times literally. The names of birth parents in New York were many times sealed with glue—never to be opened. It was incredibly difficult to get *any* information, I was told. The representative I talked with let me know that I could go ahead and fill out the contract, and that I would not have to pay a dime until the company had located my birth mother and all of my information.

I liked that deal. Not a penny out of my pocket, and I had professionals searching for me. I wouldn't have to be on the computer until all hours of the night searching every possible birth mother lead. I would be able to spend more time with the boys and Dave. "The search could take up to a year if not longer" I was informed. Bummer. That was a long time. I dug down deep, and realized that I would have to mentally and emotionally put my journey on a shelf. I could not let it consume my every waking hour. To survive the year or more search, I knew I needed to take a deep breath, trust, and wait. I wasn't good at waiting. I would have to be. Every other path had led to a dead end. This was my one hope. A possible twelve month wait. Deep breath.

The next day I downloaded the forms from the search company. I filled out all the information I had, and left many unknowns blank. It was a Thursday afternoon when I went to the post office, and faxed my contract. A Thursday afternoon at three o'clock. Done. Sent. Now to be patient and wait. I had taken my next step. Nancy Drew placed her current investigation on hold. On hold until further notice.

Chapter Eleven

It was Friday. Day one of my year of waiting for information. It was one of those homeschooling days where I didn't hop in the shower until 1 pm. No complaints. Shower was done, and I was following a routine I've followed most of my life. Normal. Ordinary.

My phone rang.

I didn't recognize the area code. Normally I just let those unknown numbers go directly to voice mail. For some reason, this time I picked up.

"Mrs. Hart, this is Joe from Kinsolving. Your case is solved. We have found your birth mother. She is living in Atlanta, Georgia. We have all kinds of information about your maternal family."

Shock.

Joy.

Back to shock.

Breathe.

"You mean it was *that* easy?" were the words that flew out of my mouth.

"Not *easy* but we found her." was Joe's response.

Back to shock again.

"As soon as you are able to wire the money to us, we will send your information to you in an email."

Twenty-three *hours. Hours.* Not days. Not weeks. Not months. Not years, but *hours.* Unbelievable. My insides were a kaleidoscope of emotions. How could she have been found so easily?

By the time I got off the phone, It was nearly 3pm. I had never wired money before. I needed that money to reach Kinsolving faster than a New York minute. (I don't know if I've actually ever *said* 'faster than a New York minute' ever before in my life.) *Fast and expedient* is how I needed money wired. By the time I got dressed, out the door, and inside our bank, it was nearly 4pm on a Friday afternoon.

I explained my predicament of needing money wired asap to the bank teller. I appreciated the whole 'are you sure this is a reliable company to send this much money to, honey' motherly advice talk I received. For a split second my stomach churned thinking about the amount of money that I was about to have deleted out of our one and only account, and I shot up a little prayer that I truly hoped this *was* all legit. Surely this company wouldn't be pulling a fast money making scheme on me. Please, oh please, no.

'Yes, ma'am, this is a good and real company, thanks for your concern". *Now can we get this moving right along?*

"I'm sorry, but there's no way that we can get the money wired today, and the banks are closed all weekend. The soonest we can

70

have it wired is Monday night. We will wire it from here Monday, but it takes a while to get processed."

MONDAY???

"Monday??? I have very important information that I need to get as soon as *possible.* Is there *ANY* way to get it there today by 5:00pm?"

I really didn't want to take the time to explain my whole adoption story to this teller, but needed her to know my urgency. I had waited forty-one years, what was another weekend, right? *Wrong!* Three more days would feel like three more years of waiting!

I was told "no". There wasn't a way. *Except* that the Walmart down the road had a Western Union desk, and might be able to get the money wired, if they were still open.

I withdrew more money than I had ever held in my bare hands. Concealed it in my purse, and headed to Walmart. *Too bad robbers and pick-pocketers...you missed a mother lode in my purse that day.*

I walked into Walmart and found the Western Union girls. Seriously, they looked barely fifteen.

"I'm sorry, ma'am, we just closed".

Seriously?

"Is there *any* way you could just quickly wire this money for me, please?"

My charms didn't work. Now if they had been young teen *boys...?* (I didn't just write that, did I?)

Back to the bank I drove. Slightly defeated. All of my information, everything that I had been searching for all those months was just a money wire away. My true identity was sitting in a cyberspace email waiting to be delivered.

I defeatedly walked back into my bank. "I'd like to make a deposit".

"Didn't you just...?"

"Yes, that was me. Western Union was closed. I guess I'll just have to wait until you can wire it for me Monday morning."

"That'll be a $35, please."

"Just take it out of my account."

I then lived the longest weekend of my life.

Chapter Twelve

Every fifteen minutes 'on the fifteen minutes' I checked my yahoo email.

"Not yet"

"Not yet"

"Not yet"

The whole day went by. FINALLY at 8:05pm, the email I had waited for my whole life (well, at least since I had discovered that I had been adopted—OK, waited four months for) arrived!

There are no classes to prepare you for reading information like I received. There were six pages of information. Where to begin? *"Let's start at the very beginning...a very good place to start...when you read you begin with A, B, C...when you sing you begin with Do-Re-Mi"*. Follow Julie Andrews' singing suggestion. The very beginning it was. Slow now. Take it all in.

My email contained six pages of information. The first paragraph restated the information I had received on the cruise. It was nice to have the affirmation that indeed I had been celebrating my birthday on the correct date. It would have really thrown me for a loop had I discovered I was born on a totally different date.

Of course there could have been forty-two years of make-up birthday parties for the correct date. That wouldn't have been too bad, I suppose. Years of missed presents...

Along the journey, I often wondered if my birth mother had named me. Was I born with a totally different name? Was it a better name than Kirsten? Was I a Pam, Christy, or Sue? Perhaps an Esmerelda, or some fancy-schmancy name. I always thought the name Kandi was cute, but with the last name Hart, I would sound more like someone on a billboard in Las Vegas. With a life in ministry, people may not look too favorably on having a Kandi Hart come to sing and speak for a Sunday morning service.

Baby Girl Murphy.

That was my name. That's who Kirsten Hart started out as. No first name. Just a description. I was a baby, and a girl. *Baby Girl Murphy.* I wonder if my birth mom had secretly named me. Was she not allowed at that time to give me a proper name? Did she choose *not* to name me? Would she have been too attached if I was named *Maria* Murphy? Kandi would have actually worked dandy alongside the Murphy name. Dang. Kandi Murphy. See, now that's a cute name.

Mother: Sue Murphy (an alias used in the maternity home). ALIAS? My birth mother used an alias on my adoption records, and she was still able to be *found?* This was unbelievable. An *alias?* How in the world were they able to trace my birth mother from an alias? '...*Trust me child...*'.

It never ceases to amaze me what God can do. I wasn't much but a paragraph into my six pages of history, and I was able to see what a miracle God had done. He destined for me to have this information. It was no surprise that *He* knew that my birth mother had used an alias.

Impossible to get adoption information? No. No impossibilities with God. His timing is different from ours in so many circumstances, but His timing is always perfect. It was time for me to see yet another miracle He had brought about in my life.

I continued reading my newly revealed personal history. I never dreamed this would be my life. Never. '*Class of 1963 University of Rochester, Rochester, NY'*. More information. CURRENT RESIDENCE AND PHONE NUMBER:

There they were. Two vital details I had been searching months for. Right before my very eyes. Her contact information. Gulp. This was really it. Her address and phone number stared at me. Want a staring match little address? I'll win, hands down. Must keep reading.

"*They are believed to have two known sons".* MORE information. Two younger brothers. I was her first-born. So I'm a first born. Now that totally messes up the psychology of the first-born personality versus the youngest/baby personality. This was really going to mess me up. Which personality do I innately have, then? I'm actually a first-born, although I was raised as the baby. Some shrink needs to put me on a couch and analyze all of this. I'd be a good case-study.

Two younger brothers. Not a sister. Wonder what they're like. Do they look like me? Mirror images, only the masculine form? Not a thing alike? Did they know about me? Baby brothers. I would have been their big sister growing up. This is a lot to take in.

I continued reading the four additional pages of information that included aunts and an uncle (along with all of *their* current addresses and phone numbers), as well as the obituaries of both of my maternal grandparents. Both of my maternal grandparents were from the Oakland and San Francisco areas of California.

Well, look who's a *California Girl* now! This was fun! Yup, "Wish they all could be California Girls...". Hello. I am! Kirsten Hart, California Girl. Nice.

'Your maternal grandfather was the Director of Advertising Services for Eastman Kodak, where he was responsible for Kodak exhibits at Disneyland, world fairs, and Grand Central Station'. Oh, how cool is *that!* My husband, Dave and I dated and fell in love at Disney World, while he was working there in 1990. And now I discover that my grandfather worked with Walt Disney in the early days at Disneyland. It really *is* a 'small world after all'. (Every pun totally intended).

My grandmother's obituary was so sweet. 'Throughout her life, she carried a love of things Californian: good friends, flowers, and produce. She created a life that embraced family, friends, and fashion. She will be remembered for her creative spirit, appreciation of beauty in the natural world, wanderlust, and eggs benedict brunches'. 'Those wishing to honor her memory are encouraged to feed hummingbirds or plant something special in their garden.' Oh, I think we would have really liked each other. I think she would have really liked me.

There were more ancestors with dates of births and deaths. One of these days I need to hire someone to research all these names. Would love to find out all about the lives of these deceased relatives. I even have names dating back to the early 1800's. I would love to know more about my 'people'. What is my heritage through all of those who have gone before me, and carry the same genetic DNA? It's all so incredible.

I read through all six pages. Then it hit me. Now what? What's my next step? Call? Write? *Call?* Would I, could I, should I? How *do* I? I immediately got online and googled my birth mother's name. I wanted to see a visual of this woman who gave me life, if indeed there was an image to be found.

I entered her name, and hit 'images'. A page full of photos popped up on my screen. There were quite a variety of birth mom possibilities. Blonde, brunettes, blue-eyed and brown-eyed women were all vying for my attention. Which one of you is my birth mother? *"Are YOU My Mother?"* Go ahead, please. Call out to me. I clicked on a few of the pictures. One was a writer for a larger newspaper. Cool. A few additional possibilities were viewed, but I didn't have a 100% gut feeling about any of my possible mommies.

My eyes shifted back to my full report. An address and a phone number caught my attention once again. What to do. If I wrote her, there's a possibility that the address I have isn't even the right address. If I wrote her a letter, it could take five to seven days to reach her. If it wasn't her, then the 'wrong address mom' could throw out the letter, and I'd never know what happened. If it was the right address, perhaps she would never write me back. If she *did* get my letter, and I had the right person, she might take a while to process it all, and then by the time she actually *did* write back, I could be going on three weeks worth of wait time.

The phone number. Phone. Number. Just looking at the numbers caused my stomach to churn. What time is it? It was 8:10 our time. That means 9:10 eastern standard time, her time zone. That's awfully late to call someone out-of-the-blue. Did I dare? '*I double dog dare you*'. This was a whole different league of dare than on the elementary school playground. This dare dealt with past issues. Adoption. Way heavier than a dare to go tell a boy you liked him. Although in elementary school, that's a pretty hefty dare. *Do I dare?*

I took the dare full on. I grabbed up my report and headed to the master bedroom. The cell phone got plugged in (so I wouldn't run out of power mid-sentence). "Hello, I believe I'm your birth daugh----". That wouldn't be good. Phone plugged in. Check. Report on my lap. Check. Butterflies churning my stomach inside out. Check. *Now what?*

I took a last minute scan of my newly read information. "Attended The University of Rochester". Hmm. That's good information to possibly start the phone conversation with. If she says she didn't attend that University? End of conversation. *"Sorry to have bothered you so late in the evening ma'am. Thank you."* And if she says she *did* attend? Gulp. Here we go. I can't believe it. Adopted? Seriously? I was adopted? And I'm about to call my BIRTH MOTHER?

Chapter Thirteen

I dialed the number.

"Hello"

It was a man's voice. My birth dad? Step-dad?

I asked for my birth mother by name.

"May I ask who's calling?"

Great. Just great.

"This is Kirsten Hart from Houston, Texas."

Seriously, that's the best you can do? That's just what came out of my mouth.

Pause.

A woman's voice came on the line, "Hello?"

This was do or die time. Rubber hitting the road. Make it or break it. The butterflies in my stomach were performing a full-on circus.

"Hi, I'd like to ask you a quick question, did you attend the University of Rochester?"

"Yes....I did".

At this point I'm sure she was thinking, 'Great, it's 9:15, and the Alumni Foundation is hitting me up for donations'.

"I'd also like to ask you if the date May 18, 1966 has any meaning or significance to you."

There. I did it. Cat out of the bag. Fully exposed. 'Not turning back...no turning back'.

"....yes..., it does..."

I then continued gently explaining a condensed version of my previous nine months.

"I think I may be your birth daughter."

"What color eyes do you have?"

"Grey, blue"

"Mine are, too. What color is your hair?"

L-Oreal Superior Preference #3 Soft Black, every three weeks. That would have been an honest response. Instead, I said, "Well, it's naturally auburn with a lot of natural curl, but there's a good amount of gray in it now"

"Mine is, too. What hospital were you born in?"

Great. Just great. The one answer I *still* didn't know!

"Well, I'm not really sure. I have a lot of information, but not the name of the hospital."

"Do you know what your birth weight was?"

That I thankfully *did* know! I was 6 pounds, 5 ounces. *Check!*

We slowly proceeded in an unraveling conversation of discovery. I indeed, *was* that little tiny baby girl she had given up for adoption forty-one years ago. I wasn't a big Twilight Zone TV show viewer, but for the hour and a half that I chatted with the woman who brought me into this world, it seemed as if I had melted into one of those bizarre Twilight Zone episodes. Where was I? Who was I? Who was I *talking to?* I had ventured into an unknown and uncharted world. One that I never dreamed would be part of my life's journey.

I additionally discovered that I truly did have two younger brothers. A year and a half after she had given birth to me, my birth mom married the man I first said 'hello' to when I called. My new stepfather knew of my existence, but not my half brothers. *Surprise! Here I am! Just call me Sissy, boys.*

We chatted longer, and I even had a chance to talk with my new step-dad. Nearing the end of our conversation, I let her know that I surely didn't intend to interrupt her life. "I know you sure didn't expect this call tonight. If it ends here, I am fine. I just wanted you to know that I am alive, healthy and happy, have a great family, and that I have had a great life."

"I have thought about you everyday since the day I had to say good-bye to you. You are family. You always have been. I would love to meet you sooner rather than later. I am so glad that you found me and called me."

There it was. Forty-one years of separation and now birth mother and daughter were reunited. *Reunited and it feels so gooood.* Well, it *did* feel good. Mostly. How will all of this fit into my previous life? I have a family. Mom, Dad, brother. They've been my *whole* family up until now. Everything's changing. Am I ready? It's exciting. Do I want all this change? Yes. No. No, yes! This is what I have been searching nine months for. Answers. The truth. Now it was staring at me in the face. It was my new reality.

I could so have my own reality show with this story line!

Chapter Fourteen

I received emails with photos the next day. So that's what my birth mom looks like. Hmmm. I think I see a little of myself in her. Unreal. I actually think I really *do* look more like my adopted mom. Seriously? There she is. And we have the same calves. Would you look at that? Same calves. My calf twin. *Can't tell we're mother and daughter? Just look at our calves. Yep. That's right. You totally see it now, don't you?!*

I received photos of both of my new nieces (beautiful teenagers), my brand new sister-in-law, and both of my half brothers. Again, not a lot of resemblance, but it was fact. I was more related to these two new brothers than anyone else in the whole world. They came out of the same womb. I was first, though. Neener, neener. I win. First place. Can't take *that* away from me, oh brothers of mine. Shoot. I wish I had a sister, too. Oh, well. I had missed out on years of being the oldest. I'm the Big Sister. This was kinda fun!

A letter came two days after my first phone call. The return address on the envelope read 'Hillside Agency, Rochester, New York'. So this was the letter with information dating back to 1965 and 1966. I had less anticipation in opening this envelope. I already knew who my birth mother was. We already had our first conversation. But, how interesting to read about her experience with the adoption agency!

I looked over the four pages of information. The woman I had talked with from the agency said that they wouldn't be able to give me specifics, but that there was a good amount of information.

I felt as though I had stepped through a time machine. Here I was, reading words that had been kept hidden for forty-one years. Amazing. Amazing that the transcripts had not been destroyed or had deteriorated in all those years. Israel found the Dead Sea Scrolls...I had my personal history from the adoption agency. Both survived. Both preserved for a purpose. Granted, the Dead Sea Scrolls were *slightly* older and of more importance, but a girl will take what she can get!

The first section re-stated the information I had received from the Adoption Registry. Age at time of birth: 24, Nationality: German and English, Eye Color: Blue, etc. I did have the additional information that my birth mother was 5'5 1/2" (I am 5'2 1/2"), that she indeed was a college graduate, her weight was _____ . (Hey, I'm a lady, and even though my document *did* record her weight then, I will respectively leave it out of this paragraph. I know when I've over stepped the line, and I'm *not* gonna do it on *this* issue. There, I feel better. No weight disclosure.) Religion: Protestant. Occupation: Personnel Department.

The only difference was that in this document, I received bit of information about my birth father: The *Mystery Man.* If you're walking though the Sahara Desert, you're thankful for even a few drops of water. I was soaking up my thirst-quenching droplets with this birth father information. *Anything* was valuable to me. This I *did* find out: Age: 24, Race: Caucasian (I pretty much could have guessed that one myself), Height: 5'8", and Occupation: *Factory?* That was interesting.

There it was. All the information available about my *father.* This is the man, that under normal circumstances would have been the man who changed my diapers, wiped my tears, and taught me about life. What did I know about him? His age, ethnicity, height, and a probable job. This person from whom I carry his DNA and heredity, I knew nothing about.

The following paragraph confirmed the fact that my birth mother had four younger siblings, 'All with blue eyes', that my grandfather was a 'very handsome man', and that my birth grandmother 'did not seem upset with her daughter, rather the situation they were in'. I breathed a sigh of relief when I read 'there is no history of mental illness in the family'. Whew. One never knows, but that was somehow reassuring to me. Except now I have excuse for any odd behaviors...

I kept reading, soaking up every syllable. Then I caught by breath. The air literally got sucked out of my lungs as I read the second sentence in the second paragraph down. *This was my life-changing moment. This is the reason why God brought me through this unexpected journey.* A few short words forever changed my life.

I'm not a very good gift *keeper.* I love to give gifts, especially to my two sons. I would give them everything if I could. It's just that when I have a good gift that I know either one of my kids would enjoy, it's hard for me to keep it from them, especially at Christmas time.

This year, for example, it was the Tuesday of Christmas week, with Christmas being on a Saturday. I had all the presents wrapped and under the tree. I just love how that looks. Only four more days to open everything when my oldest asks, "Hey, why don't we open all of the presents tonight!". *Really?*

"But then you guys won't have anything to open Christmas morning!"

"What difference does it make, it'll just be us here on Christmas. We might as well enjoy everything a little longer. Please?"

Well, I was a gonner with the *please.* Plus, he was right it was just the four of us together this Christmas. *And* it doesn't really matter the *exact day* that we celebrate Christmas, because Christ probably wasn't even *born* in December. Why not? We'll start a new family tradition of opening presents on days *other* than Christmas morning. TEAR IN BOYS!

See? It was so easy to sway me to break tradition, and go against the flow, because I so wanted my boys to enjoy what I had bought them.

Quite opposite with God. God is the best gift-keeper ever. He knows the exact perfect time to give us gifts. Not a day, hour, or second too early. It's as if God had gone to the fanciest store and had them wrap my present with the most beautiful wrapping paper, completed by an exquisitely embellished ribbon. The kind of wrapping we moms can never replicate on our own. He kept that breathtakingly beautiful package from me for forty-one years. Forty-one years until that divine moment. This was my moment. This was my gift.

My gift-sentence read, "In the Fall of 1965, your birth mother, and her mother had all the connections they needed, all the finances in place, and took a trip to the country of Sweden to obtain an abortion. After being gone for a month, they weren't able to find anyone to perform the abortion."

Abortion?

I was supposed to have been aborted?

Me?

I've lived all my life and had no idea.

I shouldn't have even been born.

I was supposed to have been....aborted?

That's all it takes sometimes. A few simple words. They can change your life. In an instant my whole past and future realigned themselves.

God had His hand on me from my days in the womb. It's a miracle I'm breathing right now. It's a miracle I'm even alive.

Oh yes, you shaped me first inside, then out;
you formed me in my mother's womb.
I thank you, High God—you're breathtaking!
Body and soul, I am marvelously made!
I worship in adoration—what a creation
You know me inside and out,
you know every bone in my body;
You know exactly how I was made, bit by bit,
how I was sculpted from nothing into something.
Like an open book, you watched me grow from conception to birth;

all the stages of my life were spread out before you,
The days of my life all prepared
before I'd even lived one day.

Psalm 139: 13-16

My world stood still while my heart spun in circles. How does a person go their whole life without this kind of knowledge? I have been able to become a wife and mother to my two amazing children only because the grace of God protected me in Sweden. *Sweden?* Abortion was completely legal there. How in the world did my abortion not go through when it should have been so easy?

Absolute miracle.

Stunned.

Grateful.

Stunned.

I get it now. I get why I couldn't find my birth certificate for the passport. I get why I felt the words, '...*find out more...*'. I get that I was born to discover this knowledge. I get that He has protected me for 'such a time as this'.

Speechless.

Eternally grateful.

Chapter Fifteen

It had been five weeks since I mailed my parents the letter. I hadn't heard a thing. No call. No letter. Silence. Were they mad, scared, upset, nonchalant? What was going *on* in their house?

I believed that I had been adopted. I had the paperwork in hand to prove that fact. Yet, it didn't seem completely real. I needed to hear the words from the lips of my mother and father, "Yes, we adopted you" to finalize my new fact. I still hadn't heard those words spoken. It wasn't a complete realization—yet.

I wanted my parents to be the ones to reach out to me at this point. They *knew*. They *knew* the fact of who I was for forty-one years. I'm the one who just found out! I'm the one who had to dig for all of this information that didn't make sense. I'm the one who sent the letter. I'm the one who was waiting for the call. I was waiting for my parents to tell me my story. I was waiting for them to comfort me. To let me know everything was going to be all right. I was waiting for my parents to 'own up'.

I never, ever, ever, *ever* thought I might have been adopted as I was growing up. Both my parents are extremely musical. That's all I knew, and I naturally gravitated towards anything and everything musical. I was always in the kids choirs at church, usually directed by either of my parents. In the forth grade, when we had to chose an instrument to play, I chose the cello.

Music came as naturally as breathing to me. It was who *I was*. And of course it should be. It was in my DNA. So I always thought.

I had a wonderful childhood. My parents were music teachers, and so when the summers came, for many years, we would go to Maine. My parents taught music students in the most picturesque setting in the southeast corner Maine. Summertime for me was swimming in the freshwater lake, canoeing with my brother, and collecting quartz rocks along the shoreline. One of my favorite memories of the summers in Maine involved blueberries. Taking a plastic bowl from the cafeteria and picking fresh blueberries. Eat two, put one in the bowl. There's nothing quite as delicious as fresh off-the-bush Maine blueberries. Actually, the fresh homemade clam chowder every Friday night in the camp cafeteria was a close runner up. There were cabins set aside as rehearsal/practice cabins scattered throughout the grounds. The sounds of violins, trumpets, pianos, organs, and every instrument created resonated gloriously through the scented pine trees of that magnificent campground. What a childhood.

I took ballet, jazz, tap, gymnastics, and cello lessons. I did all the creative, fun activities that little girls enjoy. I was loved. I was valued. I was encouraged. I was prayed over. I was blessed. I wouldn't trade my childhood for anything. It made me who I am.

Throughout my teen years, I received constant encouragement for my future. I was supported. I was driven to endless rehearsals. I was theirs. I was my parents daughter. I was taught about Jesus. I was taken to church. I was a 'church baby', there anytime the doors were open. It was my life. I didn't want to lose all those years. I didn't want anything to change between my parents and I.

Please let this be an easy transition from blood daughter relationship to known adoption daughter relations. Please let us be able to keep the beautiful past memories and flow into a new relationship of openness and peace. Please.

No, I wasn't angry, or holding in anger. I just wanted some resolution to the whole situation. *Let's get all of this out in the open, and resolve everything, and get on with our lives in a normal fashion.* I was anticipating life to resume it's standard flow. 'Here's your story. Here's why we kept it from you. You're good. We're good. Let's get on with life'. I was hoping that scenario was possible. What if everything changes? Am I ready?

I did it. I picked up my phone. The silence had gone on long enough. Let's talk. Let's get this out in the open. Let's resolve.

My mother answered the phone. Here we go. I heard an apology for not calling or writing sooner. "I didn't know how to handle this…" Then I finally heard the words that I had waited months to hear, "We adopted you when you were two weeks old". Something about the concrete fact of that statement finally triggered an emotional button in me. No going back now. I know my truth. Had the truth set me free? There were so many emotions rolling around my heart, stomach, and head at that moment, freedom was a ways off.

My parents had kept my secret for a purpose. "We never wanted you to feel that you were any less our daughter because you were adopted. I treated you as if I had given birth to you. We didn't want others to think of you differently because you were adopted." Now was not a time to rationalize. Now was a time of reconciliation. Of making things right. Of finding and searching out our new relational path.

I've never experienced what I did in that phone call. It's as if I became the mother, and my mother, the daughter. I became the comforter. I became the one who said, "It's going to be all right. It's going to be OK. I love you."

Deep down I believe that there was a voice that told my mother, "You tell her she's adopted, and she's going to leave you and go find her *real* mother". But who or what *makes* a real mother? Is she the one who gives you birth, or is she the one who teaches you about life? In most cases she's both. I, and all other adoptees fall into a separate category. We have *two mothers.* By definition, the word mother has two forms. The noun form and the verb form. The noun form: A woman in relation to a child or children to whom she has given birth. The verb form: Bringing up (a child) with care and affection the 'art of mothering'. I now indeed had both the noun and verb form of mothers in my life. Two women. Two separate forms of moms. I was talking to my 'verb mom'. My *real* mom? How odd. Two mothers.

We chatted as mother and daughter for over an hour. I hung the phone up having obtained some resolution, yet with a whole new set of questions. I needed chocolate. I needed chocolate badly.

When I told my husband, 'I was adopted when I was two weeks old', something broke. I don't believe I had shed a tear during the whole nine months concerning my adoption situation. Oh, I can easily shed a tear at the end of Extreme Home Makeover, or any Lifetime Chanel movie, but I had been on such a quest for truth, I hadn't let myself go to a teary place. There was something about the factual slap-in-your-face reality that *I WAS ADOPTED* and that I knew the exact *age and time* of my adoption that opened the emotional gate. That emotional gate wasn't open very long. I had a new question: Where *was I* for those first two weeks of life? Did I go to a foster mother? Did they keep me at the hospital? Was I kept at an orphanage? Did anyone hold me? Was I taken care of well? Did they feed me? Was I stuffed into a hamster cage in the corner of an orphanage and given one of those upside-down water bottles with the little metal ball at the end of the straw to drink my formula out of?

Chocolate. Much chocolate was needed. I must find that bag of chocolate chips.

I had received another answer during that phone call. My brother was, in fact, also adopted. We weren't related by blood at all. I could have married my *brother*. I know that sounds disgusting, but think of it. We didn't share any common DNA. No relation. Other than our name, we weren't related. Unreal. He had been adopted at three months! I would give anything to know *his* story. But, that is indeed *his story*. To this date, he doesn't have any desire to dig further and discover his hereditary. That's OK. Although, if he gave me the 'go ahead' I would search high and low to find out where he came from.

Well, the call was over. I did it. I was exhausted. I had my truth. I had more answers. I now had both a verb and noun mom. Who would've ever guessed.

Chapter Sixteen

My birth mother and I shared multiple emails and phone calls and set a date. Memorial Day weekend in five weeks would be the *second* time to meet. The first was in a hospital forty-one years ago. This time we would have the opportunity to get to know each other. To look into each others eyes, and see the bond between mother and daughter. Would that bond be there? Would I share the same bond I did with my adopted mom? Same? Different? No turning back now. This ship was set to sail.

My birth mom, step-dad, one of my half-brothers with his wife and two daughters were ALL coming to visit us for a FOUR day weekend. My brother and his family were all driving to Houston from Atlanta, and the 'folks' were flying in. Gulp. Talk about detailed cleaning! No nook and cranny went untouched. We even pulled out the washer and dryer! You know that's some intensive cleaning when the area behind the washer and dryer gets scrubbed.

The time had come. I'm surprised I hadn't lost a good ten pounds from all of the excitement and nerves combined. The day was here. We were on our way to the Houston Hobby airport. Too much traffic. Seriously, *'Houston we have a problem'* with the amount of traffic. Can't be late.

This is a once-in-a-lifetime meeting. Our friend with the good video camera was set to meet us at the airport to film the initial meeting and the first hug. Groceries were bought. Beds were made. Clean towels were hung, and new bars of soap were in the showers. Countdown.

I was facing the unknown. A whole new world lay before me just a few minutes away. We were standing at the exit gate in the airport. Thanks a lot 9/11 terrorists. Now we can't meet anyone at the gate anymore. I could have had balloons and a big sign saying, 'WELCOME BIRTH MOM' as soon as she stepped off the ramp and into the airport. Eh, perhaps this wasn't quite a balloons kind of moment anyway.

Is that her?

Nope.

Her?

Nope.

That looks like her.

Nope.

There she was.

That's her.

There's my *birth mom.*

She was wearing deep orange, which I later discovered was one of her favorite colors. Short hair, my blue eyes, my thick eyebrows, and our twin calves.

We hugged. I didn't cry. I was more slightly in shock, and so curious that I wasn't tearful. Is that weird? Perhaps on my birth *father's* side of the family there was a slight history of mental illness. Shouldn't I be weepy? I just wanted to *look* at her. I was always taught that staring at someone is rude. Permission to be rude, please.

I hugged my new step-dad, and welcomed him to humid Houston. The four of us walked down to the baggage claim together. Small talk was the order. No '*why did you give me up*' conversations while still in the airport. I've got a little bit of class, folks. My mama taught me manners. *My mama. Unreal.* My mama was right in front of me. My noun mom. My mama was also in New Jersey. My verb mom. My verb mom doesn't even know that I'm meeting my birth mom right now. Guilt? Can't even go there right now.

Breathe.

They were very sweet, this new family of mine. We had enjoyable conversation on the way home from the airport. Can one exist for hours in an outer body experience? I would venture to say 'yes'. Everything about our time together was surreal, like living two completely separate lives in perfect cohesion. Did I fit in with this family? What was my role? How was this new life going to work?

I just wanted to stare at her. *Who are you? What makes you tick? Am I you? Are we two in one?*

We brought out the photos. I, my baby pictures, high school

pictures, wedding shots, and albums of both my boys. She brought baby pictures of both of my brothers throughout their years, and heritage photos of my aunts, uncle, and relatives. Overwhelming? Slightly. Intriguing? Completely. One-hundred percent enthralling. These were my people. My *real* people. Yet, the relatives I grew up with were my people, too, kind of. Weren't they? I had had all my ancestral identity through a completely different set of relatives. Not my ancestry at all, although all of my *life history* had been with the aunts, uncles, cousins, and grandparents that I had grown up with. Two lives, one person. My new life.

My birth mom pulled out a photo of her parents on their wedding day. My grandma and grandpa. Two complete strangers. The two people who made it possible for me to come into this world. *Thank you for giving birth to your oldest daughter. For without her birth, I would never have been.* I looked at my birth grandfather's smile and hair, and I saw my Tyler. *Well look at that.* My son resembles his grandfather. And if I wasn't mistaken, I saw some of myself in my grandmother. I still think she would have liked me. I was her first official granddaughter. The first of eleven grandchildren. We could have had wonderful times out in the garden, feeding the hummingbirds. If times had only been different. Que sera sera. 'What will be will be'. It's done. Can't change a thing.

I don't remember what I cooked that evening. I guess the food itself wasn't important enough to remember, but the newly found conversations were. Catch up. Catch up on forty-two years of life. That's a lot of ground to cover.

The next day brought more discovery about each other. My birth mom wasn't musically inclined. I suppose environment really does influence a child. I was finding out that my birth family was very much artistically inclined and very creative in nature, though. I liked that fact. I leaned towards the creative in life, although in the 1990's when I tried to create dried flower wreaths and sprays, they didn't turn out so artistically and creatively appealing to the eye. Perhaps my inherited creativeness didn't come in the form of dried flower wreaths. I was OK with that.

That evening my new half-brother, his wife, and their two daughters all arrived. It was late at night, but we had their rooms ready. The adults in Ryan's room, and the girls on a blow-up up bed and couch in the game room. It was a full house. It was a family reunion. It was mind boggling.

So, you ask, are you like your brother? Um, well, he was very quiet and reserved, which made me question, 'Where in the *world* did I come from?' Games were played, food was consumed, and we were all enjoying each others company. My brother had a Border Collie, we had Shetland Sheepdogs. We had the same taste in smart sheep-herding dogs. He was all right after all. See, now I have to have a little fun with this. I *am* by the way, the *older* sister! His wife was born and raised in Mexico, and I must tell you, she made the most fantabulously uh-mazing homemade salsa that has ever reached my lips. Seriously, I told her she needed to bottle and sell her recipe.

I needed to pick up something from Hobby Lobby, so I grabbed my birth mom to see if she wanted to run the errand with me. My Dave held down the fort full of new relatives and carried on entertaining. (I owe him so much in life...)

When we were at the halfway point to Hobby Lobby, I casually asked her, "So, do I resemble my birth father at all". Up to this point, I hadn't asked, and nothing had been said about this mystery father of mine. I was dying to know *something*. "Well, I don't necessarily see all of me in your face". *Go on. Go ahead.*

Take your time. That's right, let it all out.

"I'm sure you would want to hear this grand romantic story". *Oh, yes, yes I would. Please do tell. Tell me every teensie romantic memory. Don't leave out a single detail. I want it all. Every piece of scoop. Bring it on. I'm ready. I've waited months for this. Here it is!* "Well, we didn't really have a romance". *No. That's not what I want to hear. But go ahead.* "We were both working for the World's Fair in New York City the summer of 1965," *Oh, Dave Hart, little do you know your State Fair/Circus scenario is so close. You win.* "We both worked at the Kodak Pavilion. Kodak hired your birth father from the University of Berkeley in California to run the computer system for the whole Pavilion."

HELLO! Berkeley! Smart People University! I'm so liking this. Go on..." The people our age were divided into different teams. The red team, blue team, gold team, etc. We were both on the same team. We would all hang out after the fair closed at night, and go play guitars and sing", *SING! GUITARS! A-ha! That I can relate to, although I don't know how to play a guitar. Ahh, they would sing and play guitars. How very 60's-ish. I'm so digging this!* "One night in August it was just your birth father and I that showed up after work. He was playing his guitar, and one thing led to another. It only happened once. A few months later, I discovered I was pregnant, and I told him. He said 'how do you know it's mine', and I told him of course it was his, I hadn't been with anyone else. He then left town and went back to California. I tried writing him and calling, but could never reach him, and never heard back from him."

There it was. *There was my story. The story of Kirsten Hart. Kirsten Hart's conception. Just one random night. No deep love story. Hey, count your blessings, it wasn't a rape scenario. Two consenting young adults. I do still like the guitar part. So that was it.*

No name was given. Just the fact that since I had come into her life, she had googled my birth father, and perhaps had seen a photo of him, "It was so many years ago". One other tidbit of information was dropped, "It looked as if he may have written a few computer books".

The conversation was over. I wasn't going to re-open that 'can' unless she brought it up. I had the gut feeling that what information I received was all I was going to get. End of story.

We walked into Hobby Lobby. Mother and daughter. I had my conception story. I usually always bought a bag of Circus Peanuts at Hobby Lobby (love them, but after consuming a bag, I'm good for the year). Circus Peanuts. Funny now. I was conceived at a World's Fair. It seemed fitting that I should like Circus Peanuts. Now I understood why I have such a magnetic attraction to cotton candy and fair food. I'm a Fair Baby. *Hello, I'm Kirsten Hart, conceived from a Fair. 'What Fair?' you ask, Why that would be the World's Fair, thank you very much. Much classier than a state fair. 'Why do I so enjoy cotton candy and funnel cakes?' Why, that would be because I'm a FAIR BABY! I was never given a fair chance to fight against those cravings from my beginning! It's part of who I am, friends!*

Wait a minute, the 1965 World's Fair in New York City. Isn't that where Walt Disney debuted his 'Carousel of Progress'? That's one of our favorite rides as Disney! It's all coming together and making sense now. I'm a little World's Fair baby. Aw.

I resisted the urge to buy the Circus Peanuts. That homemade salsa back at the house was calling my name. *Resist the bag with the little peanut shaped orange fluff delights. Get back to the house. It's full of guests, I mean new family.*

Chapter Seventeen

The rest of the weekend flowed smoothly. We played continuous games, and ate non-stop, just like any typical family reunion. No more talk of the birth father. We did chat about places they had lived and traveled to. We shared stories of families, and plans for life. Just. Normal.

We said our good-byes to my brother's family, and the next day shuttled my birth mom and stepfather off to the airport. We were exhausted emotionally and physically. A good exhaustion, but you know what it's like when you're hosting six people in your home for five days! I just wanted to lay around on the couch and do nothing. I started gathering towels and sheets for the laundry machine. Time to get the house back to normal. At least my house could go back to normal. My future was anything but. I now had a new mystery to solve. Just who *was* this birth father of mine?

My birth mother had dropped a few hints, but no name. He had gone to Berkeley, was from California, worked the World's Fair for Kodak, played the guitar, and supposedly wrote a few books on computers. Come on, Nancy Drew. Kick it into high detective gear.

I wasn't necessarily on the search for my 'daddy'. I already had one. I had a great dad, who fulfilled all of my father roles. I just was so curious to know who this man was that I *came from.* What if I had additional siblings? How cool would that be. Not only did I have two new half brothers, but could there possibly be sisters on my birth father's side? Since it's the male that determines the genetic sex of a baby, and since he had determined my DNA to be female, perhaps he also determined some other females? That would be so amazing. To have a sister or sisters? I never even imagined that could be a reality. I had an older brother for forty-two years. That was it. End of the sibling possibility. Not so much anymore. Who knows what awaited me out in the world. So many possibilities. Now to find him.

Once again, I was on the computer non-stop. My sons at this point were on summer vacation, so I wasn't too concerned that I was taking time away from their homeschooling to search for my long-lost birth father. Where to start my search?

I started googling photos of the Kodak Pavilion at the NYC World's Fair. I know it was a far far far shot in the dark, but I thought perhaps they may have had photos of their cutting edge computer system, and perhaps, just perhaps, a photo of the young dashingly handsome Californian that was in charge of it. No luck. I then looked at general photos from the World's Fair that were posted. Perhaps I'd see a face looking at me that would speak to me from years past. Nope.

I wrote the Kodak Company in Rochester. "Do you have employee lists of those that worked for your company at the World's Fair in 1965?" No such luck. Apparently it was against company policy to reveal the names of previous employees. I thought that was a bit odd. It had been so many years ago! Would anyone from that time really be upset that their name had been shared? Dead end.

I started to search 'Kodak employee, World's Fair NYC, Berkeley, California, computer author'. I kept switching around the wording each time, begging for a lead somewhere. I knew he had to be out there. It was just a matter of time.

I sent my birth mom the name Gary_____? I don't recall what the last name was, but his first name was definitely Gary. I asked her if perhaps this was my birth father. She said 'you are partially right'. Well, as I recall, the last name was a different and difficult name, so I assumed the 'rightness' was with the first name, Gary. That was a huge lead. My birth mom let me know that 'out of respect for the man I married after I had you, I don't want to give you the name of your birth father'. That was a little confusing to me, but I accepted it. I was sure she had her reasons, and I didn't want to push the issue. That was OK, I had the rest of the summer for my discovery process. "If you send me his exact name, I will let you know if it's him," she later emailed me. There was my carrot dangling at the end of the stick. Never had a carrot ever looked so delicious and tempting. I was determined. The search was on.

After days of searching, I had whittled the 6,957,994,850 people on this planet down to twenty names. Twenty possible fathers. Craziness, I tell you. Who searches through all the people of the world to find her father's possible name? That would be me, thank you very much. So the list contained the names of twenty men that had some kind of tie to the word California and computers. There were some Gary's mixed in with some other first names, just for good measure.

I sent off the list in email form to my birth mother's email. Then I waited. It wasn't a long wait. "He's on the list" was my return email.

"What? Are you kidding me?"

"I'm not a kidder. His name is on the list."

Do you remember the song from Fiddler On the Roof 'Wonder of wonders, Miracle of miracles...'? Well, I was singing that all afternoon. How in the *world* out of all the men in this universe would I find the actual name of my birth father? "*...trust me child...*"

I started an in-depth search of all the names on my list. I started with searching through photos of each name. Some were easily checked off when I saw their photos. Of course, I didn't have to be a mirror image of the man who gave me his genetic code, but there had to be *some* sort of resemblance.

I kept narrowing down my list. This one image and name I kept going back to. Could I be seen in that face...possibly. I took a gamble and sent a name. And his first name was indeed Gary.

'Send'. The name was sent. Would she respond? Was I getting close?

"That's him", was the response I read on my computer screen.

"You're kidding me?"

"No. That's your birth father." Darth Vader's '*Luke, I'm your father*' rang through my head. I had found him. So now what?

I bought a report of this Gary for $39.99. I thought that was a reasonable amount to find out details about this father of mine. Previous addresses and phone numbers were listed. For $39.99, I hoped that the most recent address given was his current address. You never know with these searches.

There were two additional names that came across the page of information. Two female names. Two sisters? *Sisters!* Oh, the possibility.

I didn't feel it was appropriate to make a call. I had called my birth mother, but didn't feel right about picking up the phone to call this man. A letter, perhaps would be more fitting for a man. Of course, I still didn't know if this indeed was the right Gary. I'm sure there were multiple Gary's with the same last name. Time would tell. Time, and perhaps a letter to the most current address given.

I wrote a gentle letter. I let him know about my recent adoption discovery, and that I had met my birth mom. (*Remember her?*) I gave Gary the details about the summer of 1965 that I had received from my birth mom. Surely he would remember that night! Surely...

No guilt in this letter. No "Why didn't you own up to your responsibilities with a pregnant young woman" comments in this letter. This was letter #1, an introduction. '*Hello, I'm your 42 year-old daughter. I never knew you even existed until a few months ago. Nice to meet you. Your house or mine for Christmas?*'

It was simple. I added a few photos. I wrote my return address, and his current *California* address, and positioned the stamp in the upper right hand corner. Wish me luck. 'Luck'.

Months went by. No return letter. I had sent Gary his note in the late summer, and Christmas was approaching. I mailed out a Christmas card addressed to the same house I had sent his 'summer letter' to. Spring rolled into summer, and I had heard nothing. Perhaps it wasn't the right Gary? Perhaps his wife had found the letter and torn it up before he had returned home from work? Could you imagine if I had the right name, but the wrong Gary. *'What World's Fair? I never fathered a child...did I? Is this a joke? Who put this woman up to this'?*

A full year had flown by. Another school year over. Another year older. Birthdays and holidays had come and gone, and still no word. I kept reading over that $39.99 search, and staring at the names of those two girls, my possible sisters. I had wanted to give Gary ample time to tell them about this new sister of theirs on his own terms. Better, I thought, that they find out about me by *our* father. That would be the proper way to handle all of this.

When the year mark hit, I sought the council of many friends. "What do you think, is it OK for me to try to contact my possible siblings now? Do you think that's fair? I gave Gary a full year to respond, and nothing. Do you think it's overstepping my rights to attempt to contact them? Is it right? Wrong? No? Yes?"

The overwhelming response was "If I knew that I had a sister like you, I'd totally want her to get in touch with me." "You've given your birth father enough time." "What do you have to lose?" "They may not even be in touch with your birth father. They would be so excited to know that you're their sister." Gulp.

So I started yet another search. I should open up my own agency. Kirsten Hart Private Eye. *Aye, Aye, Matey.* I looked up the first potential sister. She had the same last name as my birth father. If I even in fact had the *right* birth father. I looked up her name. Nothing. I tried her name with the addition of the word, California. Then I listed her name with California, and the words 'high school'. B-I-N-G-O. A new last name was added to hers. Ahh, she's married. My sister is married.

The place where I found her name was on the classmates.com website. In order to get on the website to see her information, I

108

had to register with classmates.com.

I registered myself under a complete alias. I listed that I had graduated from the same high school in 1984. Fake name, fake address. Good investigating skills, if you ask me. I was bound and determined to get that information. It had been a long year of waiting.

I was in. Now to dig. I put her name in the search, and to my surprise, all of her information came up, except that there was a completely unexpected detail. Her graduation year was 1983. I graduated high school in 1984. Was this a mistake? How was this daughter of the same birth father a year *older* than me? Had he been a married man?

I emailed my birth mother right away. "Not that I would care" I let her know, "But was my birth father perhaps married." And to tell you the truth, I honestly didn't care. Nothing would surprise me at this point, although I didn't think my birth mom was one that would knowingly be involved with a married man.

"If he had been, I sure didn't know about it. I never heard anything about him being married." was her response.

Had I dug too deep? Was this territory that I shouldn't have crossed into? At this point, I was ready to get it all out in to the open. No more secrets, please. The past is the past. It's done. It's gone. We can handle the truth. *'You can't handle the truth'*. Yes, I can.

I discovered through the classmates website, that this probable sister had a facebook account. I looked it up, and there was her picture. Same cheek bones. Same facial structure. Breathe....

I sent her a simple message. "Are you Gary _____'s daughter?" Her reply came. "Yes, why do you ask?" I responded with, "I just found out that I may be related to him."

Now, that wasn't too harsh, was it? It was a simple question. Was she the daughter of a man that I believed was my birth father. I could have been a long-lost niece, or a distant relative. 'Related to' could have so many different possibilities.

I had a return message. "What do you mean related to?"

There it was. My open door. What to do? What to do? Do I spill the whole bag of beans out on the table? Do I not respond, and let another year of life slip me by? Do I overstep my birth father telling her about me? What did I have to lose? My birth father, for some reason, hadn't responded back to me. What if this new sister would turn out to be the connection I always had been missing, but never knew was missing until that first hug, or first laying eyes on each other? The possibilities outweighed the negative. Jumping in feet first. All or nuthin'. Here I go.

I sent a short email explaining my past year, and the possibility that her father was my birth father. I used the phrase, "I don't mean to freak you out." Very reminiscent of the 1980's, I know. The wording seemed appropriate.

Well, that second email was the catalyst. That evening I received an email from my birth father. The first time in forty-two years and nine months (in utero) that my father communicated to me. Not the greatest message, but a message none the less.

Dear Ms. Hart:

While I have been trying to determine my response to you over the past year, it is clear the modus operandi in your quest has accelerated to disrupting people I know. This is unacceptable to me. Therefore, I am sending this information to you in hopes that it will satisfy your need and curiosity.

It is true that I worked for Kodak at the 1965 World's Fair. It further is true that _____ and I had what you described as a "one thing led to another" night. Beyond that, I had no idea of any consequences of that night until I received a letter from you.

I cannot know the motivation of your mother and father regarding their decision to not tell you of your past. I can only assume it was with the utmost love for you because in every other way it appears you have been blessed with a warm and loving home environment from your very first days of life. I hope that your discovery about your birth has not negatively impacted your relationship with your parents.

If we are related, perhaps the most important information I can pass along to you is a family health history. In the following paragraphs, I will give you a summary of health issues that might be of interest to you and your sons.

1) *My father died at the age of 54 from prostate cancer. Before the cancer, he was in excellent health. Several of his sisters died from breast cancer but at later ages (70's). Others in his family lived to late 70's and 80's and their bodies just wore out.*

2) *My mother died from congestive heart failure at the age of 80 years. She had a minor heart attack when she was 62 years old. Her three brothers suffered from cardiovascular disease. Her middle brother died at 48 from a heart attack. Both her other brothers had strokes, one at 46 years old, the other at 58 years old. Their carotid arteries were virtually blocked in both instances. They both died from heart attacks in their mid-60s's.*

3) *I have been in excellent health most of my life. When my mother died (2001), I had a body scan and subsequent nuclear stress test that found some heart artery blockage. I began taking Lipitor and a few other pills. In October, 2008, I suffered a pretty serious heart attack – 100% blockage of the Left Descending Anterior artery. Thanks to some timely work by EMTs and hospital doctors, I was treated successfully and feel fine today, although my drug regimen was increased. Further, I have been advised that avoiding stress is mandatory during this recovery period.*

As you can see, the main health risk you and your sons may face if related to me is of the coronary disease variety. I'm sure you are aware that women exhibit quite different symptoms of heart disease than men, and that the symptoms are much more subtle in women, so please take appropriate action.

The other question you seem to have concerns your musical talent – I can't carry a tune to save my life but I usually can tap my foot to a good beat without seriously hurting myself. I would think that your talent came from your environment or from another individual.

With respect to your curiosity regarding any children I might have, please understand that there is nothing to be gained by having you enter any of my family members' lives at this time even if we are related. While that might sound harsh, please respect my judgment on this issue and respect my wishes. For the best interests of all who might be involved, I ask you to withhold contacting anyone whom you think might be related to me. It will serve no good purpose and might lead to significant harm.

Please...

Finally, I think that a visit between you and I would not serve a useful purpose. From your Website it is clear we have little in common philosophically or politically. There is no reason to try to persuade me differently as this point in time. Please respect my wishes and judgment.

It would appear your life is meaningful and fulfilling. I am happy for you and wish you continued success.

Best,

Gary

That was it. After forty-two years, this is what I received. Apparently, I needed to watch out for cardiovascular problems. Check. I was grateful for the health history, but apparently, he was not very happy with me, nor did he have any desire to get to know me. Although, it did seem as though he softened up a bit from the initial greeting paragraph.

How did I feel? Mixed. Glad that at least he admitted to the 'event' with my birth mom. Glad that I hadn't had the wrong Gary this whole past year. He didn't know about me? Hmm. Seems as though he might have been experiencing selective memory. Now the heart attack in October of 2008 shot my eyes wide open. That was around the time I had sent my first letter to him. Jeez. Did my letter help bring on the heart attack? Yikes. *Talk about guilt. Nope. Can't do it. I won't accept that I was the one who brought that about. Can't go there. What if? Surely not.*

I was disappointed that he had absolutely no desire to get to know me, my husband, or his two biological grandsons. Disappointed that he didn't want me in touch with my possible siblings. Bummed. But yet grateful that at least I had *something* in my hands. How odd was my life?

During the time that I had been in touch with my older half sister on facebook, I also discovered that another possible half sister was also on the website. Interesting, this younger sister's name was Kristin. SO close to my name. I've mistakenly been called Kristin my whole life. She didn't have a full page completed for a facebook account. Just her name. No photo. My investigating skills had led me to these two women. One older. One younger.

When I had sent the email to my older sister, I also (what they call) 'friended' this Kristin. I hadn't received a response from Kristin, so after the letter from Gary, I dropped all possible future correspondence. All quiet on the home-front. This was a done and dead issue. Box it up. Put it on the top shelf. **DO NOT OPEN**. Season is closed. Adios.

I replied back to Gary's letter, and let him know that I never intended to disturb his family. That was not my nature nor intent. If he ever wanted to get a DNA test, I let him know, I would be more than willing to participate.

114

Those were the last words I sent to him, and the last words I ever received. End of story. Or so I thought.

There was no more correspondence from my older sister. There was no more correspondence from my birth father. Nine months after I received Gary's letter, I was 'accepted as a friend' to Kristin. All of a sudden she was posting photos on her facebook page, and there was all sorts of information about her popping up. She even (surprise surprise) was writing cute comments to my facebook statuses. *Now what do I do?*

My birth father had told me inexplicably not to contact anyone I thought might be a 'relative', but here was my probable half sister *communicating with me*! What would *you* have done?

She was very cute. This younger sister and I resembled each other. Not that I'm saying *I'm* so cute... I secretly showed her photo to friends, and asked if they thought we looked alike. There was an overwhelming vote of "yes"! There she was. I could look at her. So close. So very close. She posted photos of her daughter and husband. My *brother-in-law and niece.* Under normal circumstances we would all know each other. Didn't matter that I was just a *half* sister. We were sisters. We were related. We carried the same DNA. And we looked alike!

What to do, what to do, what to do. It had been nine months since Gary had asked me to not be in touch with anyone 'possibly related' to him. I had done so well. I was such an obedient long-lost unwanted daughter. I was respecting his wishes. I had sat on my non-Italian expressive hands and remained painfully quiet. All until Kristin came along. Can you imagine how I felt when she would respond with cute little comments on my facebook posts! Did she have *any* idea who I was? Did she perhaps look at my photos and think, 'Gosh, she and I look a lot alike'?

After much deliberation, I did it. I once again asked and sought wisdom with what to do. *"Is it wrong of me to get in touch with Kristen? If you were my half-sister and didn't know about me, would you want me getting in touch with you? What is the proper thing to do in this situation?"* The overwhelming vote came back, "What do you have to lose. Your birth father doesn't want anything to do with you. If I were your sister, I'd want to know about you. She has the right to know about you." Thanks, friends.

It was almost a repeat of what I said to my older half-sister. In fact, it was a repeat. "Are you Gary_____'s daughter?" was all that I wrote. Again, I wasn't completely sure if I even had the *right* Kristin. Look at the resemblance though, it was kind of unmistakable.

A response quickly came back, "Yes, why do you ask?" Uh-oh. How do I respond to *that*? If I told her the whole story, I was going against my birth father's wishes. How should I reply? *Think, Kirsten. Think woman!* I chose to not reply. I kept silent. If it was to be, it would be. Silence does not come naturally to me, but that's what I felt I should do. Shhh. I was between a rock and a hard place with this one. What was I getting myself into now?

The next day I received a message back from Kristin.

'OK, so I'm very curious to know how u know me. Particularly after your question about my father and reading your profile. Did my dad and your birth mother know each other? Who is your birth mom? Incidentally, I think it is funny our names are so similar, we are both married to Dave's and I'm not adopted, but he is....'

Oh, boy.

116

I responded.

I basically told her an extremely condensed version of what you have read in this book so far, and then added:

'Well....then this past Saturday you accepted my facebook friendship (from a year ago...), and started putting your FB account together. I was speechless, and very torn. I SO wanted to tell you everything, but your dad told me not to contact any family members. I asked you that question...because I still didn't know if I had the RIGHT Kristin.... I honestly, couldn't help seeing the resemblance. My hair is dark because underneath there is a ton of gray (I grew up a strawberry blonde!) I had a space between my teeth just like your dad's....

When I read your message this morning, I thought...perhaps now is the right time. I am torn. Even though he's not my "daddy" I didn't want to disobey your/our dad. I would love to have a relationship with him someday. BUT...when you told me that your husband is also adopted, I thought that perhaps you would understand my desire to know if I had a SISTER!!!!! (I grew up with a brother, and have the two 1/2 brothers on my birth mom's side). All of this is so topsy-turvey, exciting, and scary at the same time.

Perhaps your getting your facebook up and running was an open door to a relationship WE could have. I don't want ANY of this to be a problem in your family. I promise you I'm not some crazed maniac. It has been a huge shock to even FIND OUT that I was adopted!!! I don't know your spiritual beliefs, but I don't believe in just 'chance'. I believe there is reason and purpose to every door that is opened in our lives.

I don't know where all of this will lead. If you choose not to continue correspondence with me because of your dad, I would totally understand. BUT...I think we could have a fantastic relationship. The LAST thing I would want is problems in your family. I would be totally open to doing a DNA test if you wanted...and that is something just you and I could do together if you wanted proof.

I was amazed at the Kristin/Kirsten and marrying Dave's, too. Since finding out that I was adopted, I've thought, 'How fun would it be to have a sister?!?!? And FIND her before we're all in our 80's?!?!!?

This is now in your hands. I'm sure it's a HUGE shock. Has your husband searched for his birth family at all? It would be interesting for me to know how all of that 'went down' if he did.

Bet you didn't expect all of THIS on this Tuesday!!!'

Then she wrote:

'Hello there. When I saw your first question about my Dad it was so random in my gut I knew you were phishing for info for some reason. And I don't know why but I suspected this may be the reason. So although I am processing the info, I wasn't in total disbelief.. as I can see and understand the confusing and shocking situation you found yourself in when learning of your adoption. I can only imagine how that felt for you! I am not sure how exactly to deal with this information. If it were me, I would want to know all I could about my birth family. I would do what u have. And on my side I'm the kind who thinks if you truly are my sister of course I want to know you.

That being said, I also am close with my dad and have a great deal of respect for him. I'm also very close and feel a bit protective. I spoke with Tam today and she confirmed your contact and relayed a conversation they had. I knew nothing of it until the last 24 hrs. When I updated my fb page it was out of necessity. I believe my last login had been in 08. I had no interest until now and when I accepted your request thought maybe I knew you from high school. I HAD NO IDEA AT THAT TIME! Ultimately I need to think of everyone and must first speak to MR. GARY :-):-D before exploring this further. Thank you for honoring his request. It must have been quite difficult for you. I will be in touch.'

To which I replied:

'I totally understand, and am so thankful that you can see my side, too. From the photos I have seen of your dad, he looks like a fantastic and very fun man. I do not want to do ANYTHING to disturb your family!!! It just blows my mind to think of having a sister!

I hope you know I have been praying for wisdom with all of this for almost two years. I still can't believe it myself. I don't want any of this to affect your dad's health--and if we are to put a potential relationship aside for now--so that it won't hurt/affect him I would totally understand. It would be a bummer...but your relationship with your dad and family comes first.

I've caught myself staring at your photos. I don't know if you see it--but if you 'slapped' blonde hair on me--I think people would say we looked alike!

I am blessed with an amazingly supportive husband and the greatest teenage sons. If getting to know about the other 1/2 of who I am has to wait...life will still go on ;-). Of course...being a part of your family (in whatEVER way I would fit in) would be such a gift. I don't even know my heritage on your side of the family! Crazy...

I trust your wisdom. I just hope your dad isn't so mad at me that I am 'outlawed'...

Feel free to browse through my photo albums on facebook (there must be a 100), if you want. If we just get to know each other from afar--then I'll take it. Guess I'm a curious one by nature. Not sure if that's genetic or nurture ;-)

Let's see where this new journey takes us. (Big breath). Just have to tell you, for 43 years, I have been correcting people that my name is Kirsten, not Kristin. I've been called YOUR name my whole life!

We had a few comments back and forth about spell check on her phone. She then replied:

'Thank u for understanding and support. I can't imagine not being curious in this situation. I guess some wouldn't be but I too am curious by nature (stupid touch screen!) funny I've been called kirsten all my life! Lol! And I definitely see the similarities. Read ur email to a real good friend and he said u even sound like me!'

I responded, (and if you've ever called me by a wrong name yourself, I apologize for this next comment):

'Me=Smiling. One time in a conversation a man called me Kristin, Kerstin, and Kirsten. Yupper all THREE. Stupid people... ;-)'

Then the response:

'Just wondering, how certain are you about this?'

I responded:

'99%. I paid (gulp) $3,500 to the company to find my birth mother, and all of her information. All of that info. was dead on and correct.

When she told me about your dad, she had nothing to lose--and in fact didn't even tell me his NAME. So it makes me feel like she wasn't just making this up. In the letter your dad sent me, he confirmed that he had slept with my birth mom. That was August 1965--I was born in May 1966.

I'm totally open to doing a DNA test--even if just you and I want to do one. Believe me--this is all new and unreal to me, too.

I don't want your dad to think I want him to be my 'daddy', and make up for lost years. I have been blessed with a great dad, and have my 'father figure' taken care of ;-). I just want him to see how his DNA turned out. I'm not on the streets doing drugs...yet...and although I sucked in college computer class (in 1984)... I am FAIRLY intelligent (smile, again).

He's also got two GREAT biological grandsons, that I think he would be proud of.

(This is fun chatting with you...)'

The next morning I clicked on facebook to check if she had left me any messages. I discovered that I had been completely blocked from her facebook account. It was gone. I couldn't see any more of her photos. I couldn't read any more of her messages. Access denied.

That was almost two years ago. The last time I had any correspondence with my half sister. That door had been closed. Slammed shut.

This past Spring we were singing at an event at the Anaheim Convention Center. Not too far from where Kristin lived. I sent her a little gift of chocolate-covered strawberries, and wrote a note to be delivered with the package. *'These are some of my favorites. Thought you might enjoy them. My husband and I will be singing at the Anaheim Convention Center on Good Friday at 7pm. The admission is free. Come if you're curious. ~Kirsten'*

I don't believe she ever showed up. Perhaps she did and just sat in the back? I doubt it. No sign of a half-sister. No more messages. No more emails. Silence.

Perhaps that door won't always be closed. I am going on with my life minus my two half-sisters and my birth father. Does it affect my everyday life? Nope. Do I think about them? Occasionally. Maybe down the road in life, I'll receive a letter one day from my California family. I can only hope. It would be so wonderful. I think it would be such fun to have two sisters in my life. But until then, I'll continue to count my daily blessings, *'count them one by one'.*

Chapter Eighteen

My heart can sing when I pause to remember
A heartache here is but a stepping stone
Along a trail that's winding always upward,
This troubled world is not my final home.

CHORUS
But until then my heart will go on singing,
Until then with joy I'll carry on,
Until the day my eyes behold the city,
Until the day God calls me home.

The things of earth will dim and lose their value
If we recall they're borrowed for awhile;
And things of earth that cause the heart to tremble,
Remembered there will only bring a smile.

CHORUS
But until then my heart will go on singing,
Until then with joy I'll carry on,
Until the day my eyes behold the city,
Until the day God calls me home.

What precious words: But until then my heart will go on singing, Until then with JOY I'll carry on. Carry on indeed. Life is sweet and beautiful. What a gift it is! I am so blessed with the most precious husband, and the two greatest sons a woman could wish for.

God *'gave me a story'* when I least expected it. Some may look at what has transpired in my life as a trial. A test. *"God must be trying to teach me something. That's why He's giving me this test".* Have you ever heard someone say that, or thought it about your own life? As if God isn't so pleased with you, and is bound and determined to 'learn you a lesson'?

I don't see God that way.

I know plenty of teachers. Teachers who give tests to their students on a regular basis. What good teacher would ever give his or her pupil a test to 'learn 'em a lesson'? Teachers prepare their students so that they are completely ready to pass a test with a 100% A+ grade. Only a bad teacher would give their students a test they weren't prepared for.

How much greater of a teacher is our heavenly Father? He is all loving. As Matthew 7:10-11 states. "Or if they ask for a fish, do you give them a snake? Of course not! If you, then, though you are evil, know how to give good gifts to your children, how much more will your Father in heaven give good gifts to those who ask him!"

God isn't in the business of wanting to teach us lessons so badly that He wouldn't give us the tools, like any good teacher, to pass that test with flying colors. Trust Him! He's already taught you *everything* you need to know to take whatever test comes your way. You have the notes, you've done all the necessary bookwork

124

and reading. Get though the test, pass it with an A+, and look forward to your next chapter! God has new and more exciting chapters in your life, but you can't get into those new areas of learning until you get past that last chapter. The future is bright.

I've decided to count everything that has happened to me as a blessing. It's the *only* way to exist. Choose joy! Be positive. Trust that God knows your steps, and has a better path prepared for your life than you could ever imagine.

Do I still have unanswered questions? Yes. Do I dwell on them? No. It's not worth my time.

My parents and I have a great relationship. I have *chosen* that path. I love my mom and dad. I wouldn't be who I am today without them. Adoption was such a beautiful gift for me. It's as if God saw everything I was supposed to be while I was just two weeks old, and thought, '*I have just the perfect family for Kirsten. This family will love her unconditionally, and all the gifts I have poured into her will unfold under their gift of parenting.*' We adopted kids can turn out all right! I thank God for who He chose as my parents.

My relationship with my adopted mom continues to blossom. I am indebted to her for the rest of my life. I wouldn't exist without her ultimate sacrifice of birthing me into this world. She endured a life of hidden shame so that I could exist. What an amazing gift. What an amazing woman.

I was indeed *The Secret Child.* My birth mother didn't know the secret of who was raising her baby girl, and she kept the secret of my birth all of her life. My parents kept my adoption secret from my brother and I. My half-brothers didn't know about their 'secret sister', and I have a whole birth father family to whom I am still very much the *Secret Child.*

My story is not complete. I still have chapters to write, but for now this is the story God has given me to share. It's His story of love, grace, and forgiveness though my life's steps. The path He has chosen for me.

What is *your* story? Are you sharing what God has done in your life with others? They are waiting. Your life's story is given to you for sharing and for the encouragement of countless people. Walk in your path, and enjoy the journey.

The End... And Yet The Beginning

Contact Kirsten Hart

If you are interested in Kirsten coming to speak for your church, organization, retreat or conference, please contact her through her website:

www.kirstenhart.com

or email:

kirstenhartspeaks@yahoo.com

Along with sharing this story for groups, she also has a variety of other speaking topics available.

Made in the USA
Charleston, SC
18 October 2013